The High School
Scene in the Fifties

The High School Scene in the Fifties

Voices from West L.A.

BONNIE J. MORRIS

BERGIN & GARVEY
Westport, Connecticut • London

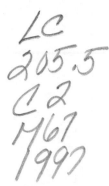

Library of Congress Cataloging-in-Publication Data

Morris, Bonnie J., 1961–
    The high school scene in the fifties : voices from West L.A. /
Bonnie J. Morris.
       p.   cm.
    Includes bibliographical references and index.
    ISBN 0–89789–494–4 (alk. paper)
    1. High school students—California—Los Angeles—Social
conditions—Case studies. 2. Jews—Education (Secondary)—Social
aspects—California—Los Angeles—History—20th century.
3. Gentiles—Education (Secondary)—Social aspects—California—Los
Angeles—History—20th century. 4. Sex role—Social aspects—
California—Los Angeles—History—20th century. 5. Social
structure—California—Los Angeles—History—20th century.
6. Nineteen fifties. 7. High school graduates—California—Los
Angeles—Interviews. I. Title.
LC205.5.C2M67 1997
373.794′94′0954—dc20   96–41449

British Library Cataloguing in Publication Data is available.

Library of Congress Catalog Card Number: 96–41449
ISBN: 0–89789–494–4

First published in 1997

Bergin & Garvey, 88 Post Road West, Westport, CT 06881
An imprint of Greenwood Publishing Group, Inc.

Printed in the United States of America

The paper used in this book complies with the
Permanent Paper Standard issued by the National
Information Standards Organization (Z39.48–1984).

10 9 8 7 6 5 4 3 2 1

for my parents and my parents' friends,
who raised me with humor and intelligence

and for my writing mentors, Toni Armstrong Jr.
and Henry Walker, who reminded me to listen
to the stories of others

Contents

The doors swing open on a new school term. You're back, and you--but there come Bev and Bud! You catch their conversation.

"Hiya, Bev!" Bud calls. "Say, where did you get that swell sun tan?"

"Down on the farm," Bev replies. "You're looking A-1 yourself, Bud. Working at the filling station must have been good for you."

"Heck, I thrived on it!" Bud grins. "Have you seen Pat this morning?"

"Yes, she and Tom are in the office, arranging a senior class meeting. Lucky, aren't we, to have those two as our class leaders?"

"You can say that again! Tom's as fine as they come, and Pat--well, it's no wonder she's so popular."

You eye them enviously as they walk down the corridor. That's the way you want to be--friendly and self-confident, like Bev and Bud; admired, like Tom; popular, like Pat.

Okay. You have the same chance they had.

--Gay Head, *Hi There, High School! How to Make a Success of Your Teen Years*

Introduction: Contexts of Ethnicity, Gender, and Friendship

This is the story of seven friends who came of age in West Los Angeles in the 1950s, as students simultaneously sheltered from and exposed to changing frameworks of democracy that would soon produce the civil rights movement and campus protests. Through the medium of oral history, the memories of this one group present a strong argument that the 1950s were more than years of dutiful obedience to the status quo. Despite the ever-present risk of social ostracism, these individuals were willing to push beyond conformity, crossing barriers of gender and ethnicity in their personal defiance of codes for young people.

As the initiator of this study, I chose to reveal a previously untapped social history because its principal actors are persons whose stories--and political choices--literally shaped my life. This is, among other things, the history of my parents.

I began to formulate an academic interest in my parents' adolescent lives when I was twenty-eight and enjoying my first appointment as a university professor. Teaching California history and American ethnic history at California State University-Chico, I found that many of my students came from Los Angeles, where I had been born and lived until the age of ten. Yet none of these students were Jewish and certainly none shared my conviction that Los Angeles was a significantly Jewish hometown. Chico, in fact, turned out to be the first community I'd ever lived in without a visible Jewish population, and I was acutely aware of being alone in my ethnic identity. I had just completed six years of graduate school in New York, and the Yiddish slang terms and patterns of speech I had used casually during previous semesters of adjunct teaching now fell flat in my Chico classroom. Furthermore, it never occurred to my Chico students that I might *have* a Jewish heritage. With the Welsh/Norwegian looks I had inherited from my non-Jewish father, I blended in well with the athletic

Protestant physiques on Chico's campus. Yet no one in town *looked like my mother*. Hers was the face I invoked to bless and protect me as I became witness to many anti-Jewish jokes.

In this environment, with the peculiar intensity of one who had just completed her Ph.D. in U.S. women's history, I developed a retroactive fascination with the circumstances that led my parents to "intermarry" in 1959. Considering the range of subtle to overt disapproval still shown toward multicultural couples today, in these presumably more enlightened times, I marveled at the daring my own parents surely exhibited in the face of earlier social codes. With tape recorder in hand, I flew home to interview the still-notorious couple Myra and Roger, who were then celebrating thirty years of a marriage many had predicted would collapse due to "difference."

In the course of recording my parents' testimony on social boundaries in 1950s Los Angeles, I spoke with many of their old friends, who surfaced as willing witnesses to the period. The result was an astonishing outpouring of wry nostalgia and criticism, the raw material for a narrative photograph of high school pecking order. The adults I had loved and known since childhood as "my parents' friends" now took on new shape as active, living texts. Their ability to transform into earlier, younger selves--teenagers who had been alienated immigrants, rebellious independents, risk-taking "fast girls"--gradually generated the oral history of a diverse collective: seven high school friends who came of age together and are in touch to this day. It is with profound gratitude for the memories and trust of the persons who have known me since babyhood that I present these voices from the Fairfax High and Los Angeles High School legacy of caste and cool.

ETHNICITY, GENDER, AND FRIENDSHIP

When the teen advice author Gay Head wrote *Hi There, High School!* in 1953, the United States was still riding its crest of victory from World War II. The forthcoming Supreme Court decision on *Brown v. The Board of Education* had not yet sounded the death knell for legal racial segregation in American public schools. The powerful new medium of television, in its infancy, broadcast no news analysis critical of domestic policy, for the *Red Channels* guidelines produced by the House Un-American Activities Committee would brook no suggestion that postwar America was less than a powerful Christian democracy.

In short, an oppressive mantle of denial cloaked the social and educational institutions from which one might expect a healthy process of cultural criticism. Under such circumstances, no high school reading curriculum hinted at the issues of racism, class conflict, religious intolerance, and premarital sexuality. Yet these conditions were very much present in students' lives. Collectively, psychologically, they informed the high school experiences of my parents, Myra Schiller and Roger Morris, and their closest friends in postwar Los Angeles.

Ethnicity

My parents' intermarriage was controversial in its day. A Jewish/Gentile union, though certainly not unheard of in the increasingly secular and assimilated climate of Jewish L.A., nonetheless sent out bells of alarm to the many folk who supported ongoing social segregation. By the Depression years of the 1930s, when my parents were born, Jews were by no means underdogs in the burgeoning entertainment industry of Hollywood; yet throughout America, restrictive covenants in real estate and quotas for Jews at prestigious universities were constant reminders of the Aryan ceiling. After World War II, the reality of institutionalized anti-Semitism in America was exposed to an embarrassed public through the 1947 film classic *Gentleman's Agreement*. Social and business club associations, fraternities and sororities, hotels, resorts, attractive new residential suburbs, and certain job markets remained closed, in varying degrees, to those with Semitic names and facial features. Although wartime revelation of the Nazi death camps linked anti-Semitism to genocidal horrors, temporarily shaming overt Jew-baiters in America, the Cold War years which followed Allied victory soon reintroduced propaganda stressing Jewish communism and Jew-as-traitor, tragically culminating in the Rosenberg trials. The 1950s were anxious years for American Jewry--a population whose ranks had, not incidentally, swelled with arriving Holocaust survivors and other refugees from Europe.

Socially, therefore, Jews and Gentiles moved in separate spheres in postwar L.A., regardless of both groups' opportunities for upward mobility. The economic incentives attracting East Coast and European Jews westward before, during, and after World War II included business security in a seductive, sunny climate. With expansive beaches, a studio-based movie empire quickly spilling over to television, and a state economy boosted by postwar military contracts to excellent research universities, Southern California was no hardship post. The glamour of having a colleague or a family member in the film industry and the easy mixing of Jews and Gentiles in public schools enhanced L.A.'s appeal to families with West Coast kin. Aware that they would never be members of, say, the Jonathan Club on Pacific Coast Highway, Jews still found in Southern California an accepting America--an America which, as historian Alice Kessler-Harris has said, "held out the possibility of love and satisfying work."[1]

As the map of Jewish L.A. expanded to incorporate formerly all-WASP middle class neighborhoods, school districts on the West Side filled with Jewish children who were first- and second-generation Americans. Their exposure to more settled Gentile classmates and, in turn, the exposure of non-Jews to industrious immigrants created a remarkable era of beneficial tension. No longer could Jews be written off as "other," as "dirty," as "foreign," when they quite willingly adapted to the California youth culture epitomized by drive-ins and beach parties. The function of public school as an institution for "normalizing" and assimilating cannot be overestimated; yet even as students happily adjusted to one another's cultural signifiers, the separate social realms of adult society made interethnic dating taboo. If the job of the high school was to prepare youth for adult mores and realities, then the social parentheses based on ethnic differences could not be ignored.

Consequently, West L.A. high schools such as Fairfax and Los Angeles High --both heavily Jewish throughout the 1940s and 1950s--carefully adhered to social conventions by establishing separate social clubs for Jewish and Gentile students. In the era where social club rushing served as a precursor to fraternity, sorority, or debutante identity in the adolescent's coming young adulthood, both male and female high school clubs were strictly divided along the Jewish/Christian line. The colorful names and histories of these social clubs-- the Tantras and Donatellos, the Cardinals and Barons, the Dantes, Vogue, Sans Souci, the Zephs--in fact masked a pecking order that was often determined by parents and school officials, as well as by privileged students.

Up until junior high, the social selection process was kept to a minimum in schools dedicated to the inculcation of democratic ideals. By the age of thirteen, however--not coincidentally the corresponding age for Jewish youths' *bar* and *bat mitzvot*--students preparing to enter Fairfax or L.A. High began to anticipate club bids from the appropriate organizations, and to dream of being accepted into a "top" club. Absurdly, yet predictably, the wooing of junior high students for high school club rushing was based in part on the thirteen-year-old's looks and social savvy. Some students graduating from eighth grade into the new world of high school and club life knew full well that old friendships would be severed by the double-edged scalpel of popularity and ethnic alliance.

Theoretically, no Jew was invited to pledge a Gentile club. Such an embarrassing error was delicately prevented by agents of the high school principal's office, who supplied names of Jewish students to the Jewish rush chairs, and names of (white) Gentile students to their club rush counterparts. The existence of alternative club phenomena for the high schools' Asian, Hispanic, and black students remains unconfirmed. Socially, everyone knew that the club world was split between Jews and white Christians. And within each hemisphere ran an even more complex hierarchy of "top" club, second-best, and, among girls' clubs, "dogs."

Those students who dared cross over into a club location to which they were not born fell into three groups: students of mixed Gentile/Jewish background, who were forced to choose a social allegiance at puberty; Jewish students attempting (successfully) to pass for WASP; and rebels thumbing their noses at the entire business. My father belonged to this latter group. Growing up the lone Gentile among his Jewish playmates, he saw no sensible reason to abandon loyal gang ties upon entering Fairfax High, and with maverick complacency became the only Gentile in the hip Jewish Cardinals club. It was, at that time and place, a revolutionary choice--yet born of actual belief in the democratic ideals so often parroted in 1950s curricula.

Still, few who witnessed the fondness of the Cardinals for their *goyische* mascot would have bet on Roger's happy marriage to a Jewish girl. The strongest taboo was not fraternal interaction but sexual mixing. For a Gentile to date a Jew was a step down in terms of racial purity; for a Jew to date a Christian was also a step down. Furthermore, it was a step *away,* a mark of disloyalty to tradition and to the Jewish family. Nevertheless, my parents, both reared in this climate of social separatism and suspicion, fell in love and planned to marry. Their willingness to endure subsequent ostracism and intrusive questions from all sides made them rebels of the most romantic kind, Shakespeare's own star-crossed lovers. And so their home communities, steeped in mutual ethnic bias, waited captiously for the hybrid baby from this intermarriage, the half and half daughter that is me.

Gender

Beyond any other implied or apparent function, high school clubs played a crucial part in sex-role socialization, as well as reinforcing ethnic groups' interpretations of gender. In terms of actual club mores and activities, there was a vastly greater difference between male and female realms (across all club levels) than between Jewish and Gentile structures therein. As religious and ethnic demarcations were obsessive qualifiers in Los Angeles business and social circles, gender identity informed nearly every act for young people coming of age in the 1950s.

This era in United States social history has been a perennially favorite subject for sociologists, novelists, and filmmakers, beginning in the early 1970s. Witness the tremendous popularity of the 1973 film *American Graffiti,* its successful television spinoff "Happy Days," and the film adaptation of the Broadway musical hit *Grease* later in 1978, all examples of the fifties craze marketed to popular culture enthusiasts and nostalgic consumers.

Yet this fondness for an era gone by had more to do with white male America's longing for carefree supremacy than with genuine conviction that the years of segregation and McCarthyism posed answers to present American problems. While male film producers and radio disc jockeys turned "oldies," and their accompanying scenarios, into marketable curios for the next generation, adult women who had grown up with the behavior codes of postwar America exploded myths of willing conformity in one feminist novel after another.

Why were the 1950s such a limited, reactionary decade for women and girls? The Northeastern University sociologist Wini Breines explored this question in her 1992 book *Young, White and Miserable,* but the historian's starting point should be Connie Field's 1975 documentary *The Life and Times of Rosie the Riveter.* In this remarkable film, long a staple of university women's studies courses, we see World War II newsreels urging women into wartime blue-collar work, juxtaposed with modern-day interviews with former Rosies--an effective documentary on American women's contributions to the war effort as the need for industrial labor power opened up jobs once restricted to men. Yet the film goes on to demonstrate the U.S. government's industrial about-face as veterans returned to seek work in the burgeoning postwar economy. Swiftly, women were returned to the kitchen. While many went willingly, others with strong new skills who desperately needed ongoing wage security were summarily cut off from the unionized job market.

Within a five-year period, therefore, women attained previously unthinkable heights in job training, public participation, salary, and occupational self-confidence, only to have their ascension into national production work quickly written off as an emergency aberration. With the return of victorious men who had long been separated from wives and sweethearts, a manic era of domestic resettlement began, resulting in the demographic baby boom, suburban housing development, and a fresh emphasis on traditional sex roles within Cold War ideology.

For young women in the 1950s, the dearth of alternatives and the valorization of virginity were institutionally enforced. High school graduation did not segue into adult freedom for college-bound women, as those universities which did admit women practiced in loco parentis parietals restricting female living arrangements and dating. Curfews, chaperones, and countless dormitory regulations imprisoned and infantilized college women, whereas their male peers might freely enjoy later hours, off-campus apartments, smoking in public, and unlimited dating. As Thomas Pynchon commented in his introduction to Richard Farina's classic beat novel *Been Down So Long It Looks Like Up To Me,* university codes mirrored parental and community values in safeguarding female virginity.

1958, to be sure, was another planet. You have to appreciate the extent of sexual repression on that campus at the time.
...At Cornell, all undergraduate women were supposed to be residing, part of the time under lock and key, either in dormitories or in sorority houses. On weeknights they had to be inside these places by something like 11 p.m., at which time all the doors were locked. Staying out all night without authorization meant discipline by the Women's Judiciary Board, up to and including expulsion from school.
...Landlords and local tradesfolk were also encouraged to report to the Administration the presence of co-eds in off-campus apartments.[2]

Few middle-class white women in the 1950s lived on their own before marrying, more typically moving directly from their parents' home into married housekeeping, with perhaps a brief period in a supervised girls' dormitory at college. A young woman went from being so-and-so's protected daughter to an eventual "adult" identity as Mrs. Somebody. Seldom was there any separate existence not linked to a man. This gendered phenomenon of being a person by association is crucial in understanding the limited playing fields for young women's individualism. Where a young man's "coolness" went in many directions, defined by his car, his prowess in sports, his stature as a beach figure, his reputation in the minor vices of gambling or drag racing, women demonstrated coolness by dating Mr. Cool.

Even the celebrated beatnik alternative of the 1950s produced a literature notoriously sexist in its depiction of female nonconformity. Female characters in beat novels exhibit a purely sexual quality, a prurient availability enjoyed by the principal beat males. In this sense beat literature was fairly hegemonic, since according to mainstream society, a young woman who sought her own pad either had been disowned by her family or was looking to entrap men: such was the prevalent logic which made it difficult for "nice" girls to obtain rentals from suspicious landlords. That young women might seek a private loft for the same artistic work male beats pursued should have been a theme in beat literature; it was not. There was no respect for the concept that a countercultural woman was herself a searcher or an artist whose intelligence, whose degree of talent, made it difficult for her to conform to the prescribed female role of the 1950s.

Instead, writers such as Jack Kerouac implied that a "chick" was a "groovy chick" not because she did anything of artistic merit, never because she espoused opinions of merit, but because she was willing to sleep with groovy guys. This is evident in Kerouac's 1958 novel *The Dharma Bums*. Observe the dialogue in the following passage, where the male protaganists are planning a Zen Buddhist backpacking trek for meditation and enlightenment. A young female friend of theirs expresses her desire to join this pilgrimage.

She'd inquired about our plan to climb Mount Matterhorn and said "Can I come with ya?" as she was a bit of a mountainclimber herself.
    "Shore," said Japhy, -- "Shore, come on with us and we'll all screw ya at 10,000 feet," and the way he said it was so funny and casual, and in fact serious, that the girl wasn't shocked at all but somewhat pleased.[3]

Because nonconformity, in women, was linked to sexual promiscuity in many men's imaginations, how a woman behaved in bed overshadowed her possible intellectual achievements. Carolyn Cassady's 1990 book *Off the Road* addresses her years as traveling companion to Jack Kerouac and wife to Neal Cassady, and sheds some light on the hierarchy of male trend setters and female beatnik camp followers in 1950s counterculture. Few women won the political attention reserved for their male peers. Power and influence for nearly all women in the 1950s lay in relationships, not achievements.

With this social scenario in mind, it becomes easier to understand why adolescent girls willingly conformed to school structures granting them agency, even in loathsome contexts. In the West L.A. system of high school clubs, sixteen-year-old girls decided who was good enough to receive a club bid and implemented these often cruel decisions with little adult intervention (adults having already set in place the ethnic restrictions for club rushing and membership.) Society might instruct the values of beauty, femininity, popularity; but in the school hallways it fell to teen minions to enforce and uphold that status quo. In no other institutions would young women enjoy such power, beyond the private clubs or school boards many joined as adults. The political power to include and exclude could be savored with temporary relish during the years of high school pecking order. Not surprisingly, while male hazing rituals stressed drinking or acts of physical endurance and discomfort, girls' clubs such as Vogue initiated new members through rites of personal humiliation and public embarrassment--demanding a harsh, false intimacy rather than physical heroism.

Girls' clubs stressed a glamorous, rather than sexual, look for members. Glamour was an acceptable excess of style in the local culture informed by Beverly Hills and Hollywood. *Sexy,* however, as one interviewee declared, was dangerous, stereotyped as lower class, feared as an impediment to well-timed marriage under well-organized circumstances. The expected competition for boys encouraged dishonesty between female friends; no one was truly certain what her friends did or felt, for to speak openly of desire or to admit to acting on that desire meant certain destruction of one's reputation.

For young men, the famed double standard allowed not only sexual experimentation, but exaggerated boasting of one's worldly experiences (rather than cover-up and/or denial). The postwar mythology of teenage boys as phallic hoodlums with uncontrollable urges dovetailed with teachers' lectures to high school girls: moral influence, in a good girl, meant taking the responsibility for keeping boys' urges at bay. Thus boys' clubs permitted all manner of free-wheeling recreational vices, while girls' clubs emphasized service, virtue, manipulation, and preparation for marriage.

Friendship

The seven old friends who speak herein--Roger, Myra, Pat, Jennifer, Bob, Helen, and Sue--provide startling glimpses into the process of self-creation during an era of rules. Individually, they represent a microcosm of familiar high school stereotypes not limited to the 1950s: good girl, "fast" girl, All-American guy, scholarly Jewish bookworm, and so on. Collectively, their perceptions and skilled use of irony--and the fact that they have remained friends--empowers this retelling of scenarios long past.

Through school, family associations, and friendships, these male and female adolescents in West L.A. met one another and began the complex rituals of dating. Considering the very different worlds reserved for each gender, the possibility of a permanent life together--marriage--intimidated many. Both

Jewish and Gentile boys at Fairfax and L.A. High often adopted pretentiously streetwise argot, asserting the illusion of experience. Girls, encouraged to believe that it was not well-bred to discuss actual family crises or emotional problems (an artifice eventually challenged by the consciousness-raising groups of the women's liberation movement), learned to speak vapidly, to be good listeners to the male monologue, perhaps inserting moral guidance at appropriate points. While male/female conversation was a necessary prelude to physical intimacy, it was also burdened with each gender's socially cultivated ignorance about the opposite sex. A society obsessed with the significance of girls' premarital virginity could not afford to encourage easy friendship between the sexes. And yet such platonic friendships, where they bloomed, served an important function for genuine honesty and insight.

In the 1980 film *Diner,* set in 1959 Baltimore, we see a group of young Jewish males wrestle with the question, What do you talk about with your wife after you marry? For the male characters, easy, intimate conversation flows during their nights at the Fells Point Diner, an identifiably but not exclusively male space--a step beyond, say, a high school students' drive-in. The pivotal film characters include recently married, "trapped" Daniel Stern and nervous groom Steve Guttenberg. In one scene Stern notes that only through marriage proper do amorous young couples find the social sanction to have sex; yet now, married, permitted free and spontaneous sexual expression, he and his bride are unable to sustain a conversation--their courtship talk having revolved around where, when, and how to arrange clandestine premarital intercourse. Stern's character is shown harassing his young wife (Ellen Barkin) for her allegedly careless treatment of his precious jazz records when she fails to appreciate their significance or to share his joy in record label trivia. The film supports the perspective that men have but a short time to enjoy free fun with the boys before married life pins them down on the domestic butterfly board. In *Diner,* Steve Guttenberg's character is so ambivalent toward his own wedding that he gives his bride-to-be a football trivia test which she must pass (proving *her* fluency in *his* world) in order to marry him. She fails on a technicality, but the film concludes with their marriage (the men all wearing yarmulkes as a symbolic reminder to the audience that this is *Jewish* Baltimore). And Guttenberg concedes that perhaps one really didn't need to be able to talk to one's wife about football, or cars, or jazz records, since "You've always got the guys at the diner."

The exclusion of men and women from one another's primary social lives during the 1950s is probably a contributing factor to many failed marriages and divorces of the 1960s. Nevertheless, the collective experience of attending high school at a certain time and place makes for lifelong connections across marriages, across gender, as graduates reflect on that group experience of adolescent subordination to schooldays. In the following interviews, the male and female interviewees report similar impressions of high school structure per se, but are astonished by one another's revelations of male versus female rites

of passage.   Their overtly gendered adolescent foundations create frequent
contradictions within the group's recollections; yet the voices are all distinctively
West L.A., united by that common social and regional reference point.

Returning to one's high school years is potentially strong magic; for some,
high school is the most prevalent metaphor of youth. That we dare to reconjure
those days suggests both bravery and folly. Do we really change? Out of respect
for the changes my parents' friends have undergone, and their privacy as
professionals, some names have been altered in this text.

Nostalgia for the American 1950s continues to feed a commercial culture and
perpetuates affection for homogenized images such as the Bev and Bud
characters of *Hi There, High School!*--blond, wholesome, WASP adolescents.
This is not about Bev and Bud. For in West L.A., the high school seniors were
just as likely to be named Cookie Metz, Ada Finkels, Teddy Lipschitz, Seymour
Weisberg, Charnette Firestein, Myra Schiller. And the postwar Americanization
agenda affecting both Jew and Gentile in high school has been, for too long, a
missing page of the social history yearbook.

NOTES

1. See Professor Kessler-Harris's introduction to the 1975 Persea Books reissue of
Anzia Yezierska's 1925 classic Jewish immigrant novel, *The Bread Givers*.

2. Thomas Pynchon, introduction to *Been Down So Long It Looks Like Up To Me*,
by Richard Farina (Penguin, 1983), p. vi.

3. Jack Kerouac, *The Dharma Bums* (Penguin, 1958), p. 24.

THE INTERVIEWS

Of course you want to be popular. Everyone does. Everyone likes *to be liked*.

Then what's the secret of popularity? What will make you *likable?* And how do you "get that way"?

You know the secret of popularity isn't beauty or money or a bundle of brains, because you see plenty of examples to the contrary.

There's Jane. She isn't beautiful. In fact, she's almost homely in looks. But Jane's popularity plus. Why? Because she has a friendly smile for everyone and she's always ready to pitch in and help get a job done.

Ted helps support his family, so he doesn't have much spending money. But Ted's well-mannered, considerate of others, interested in everything that goes on at school, and always in a good humor. He's Number 1 on the date parade.

Phoebe isn't a brain-box but she's a good dancer and a good conversationalist and, when she talks, she "makes sense." Phoebe gets around.

--Gay Head, *Hi There, High School! How To Make A Success of Your Teen Years*

1

Roger

Roger was one of the gods of his adolescent world. Athletic, intellectually precocious, strikingly handsome, a model and sometime extra in Hollywood movies since babyhood, he made quite an impression on those who met him in the 1950s. Admirers described him as "gorgeous," "stunning," "a major stud." Enjoying the considerable freedoms accorded to young white males of the middle class, Roger spent his teen years bodysurfing, cruising Hollywood Boulevard, and pursuing mild gang activities with his friends. Yet loyalty to his Jewish childhood buddies also led Roger, a very Gentile heir to Welsh and Norwegian bloodlines, to join an all-Jewish club at Fairfax High--the Cardinals--thus sealing his reputation as an eccentric line-crosser. In his final film role at the age of seventeen, appearing with his younger sister, Pat, in the opening scenes of *The Day the Earth Stood Still,* Roger may be clearly observed fleeing the alien space ship in his Fairfax Cardinals club jacket.

Roger eventually married a popular Jewish girl from L.A. High, Myra Schiller, and thus, according to standard religious interpretation, fathered Jewish children. This gesture toward biculturalism was considered unusual in a Gentile male adolescent. Handy with Yiddish humor and quite familiar with American Jewish culture, Roger was mistakenly identified as a Jew in many Jewish gatherings. Yet once married, he entered a unique social location, aware that his own wife and two children occasionally experienced anti-Semitic comments which did not apply to him.

The Gentile who grew up to become my father is an enthusiastic talker, who enjoyed recalling his youthful exploits in Southern California. The following oral history emerged whole cloth one night when Roger was entertaining a guest at our family home. These stories appropriately set the stage for perceiving the vast gulf between male and female adolescent culture in West L.A. after World War II.

The beach: the thing that made my adolescence was the beach. Now, the beach could be gotten to in a couple of different ways. If you knew somebody with a car, that was the way to get to the beach. But up until I became best friends with Mel, who was older and had access to his mother's car, I didn't have any wheels. Now one way you could get to the beach was to take the bus--ten miles, fifteen maybe, straight down Wilshire Boulevard or Olympic Boulevard. But the bus was déclassé. You tried to do anything else you could. So what we would normally do was hitchhike to the beach. And we would have adventures.

Because every once in a while you'd get picked up by a weirdo, okay? The folklore among us kids was such that we all knew about these guys, and we knew how they acted and we had information as to how to behave with them. The idea was if you kind of went along with them they would go out of their way to take you places. In California the land ends in a series of palisades and down below is the Pacific Coast Highway and on the other side of the highway is the beach. Normally, if you took the bus or hitchhiked you were let out at the palisades and had to climb down, which was okay, but it was hot and dirty. If someone would *take* you all the way down to the beach, that was a big deal! So if you were nice to one of those overly friendly guys, you know, they would take you any place that you wanted to go. But the important thing was that once you had intimated that you would do whatever he wanted, you had to jump out of the car and run. And so we got pretty good at that. And I had my share of being picked up by perverts, and we all did, and we all exchanged stories, and our lore improved, and our prowess improved, and our ability to get to the beach faster than the bus improved. We were street-smart. Well, not anything like New York kids, but for our little area we were street-smart.

There were certain things you did at the beach. Number one on the hit parade was body-surfing. Body-surfing was where it was at, and that was the thing that you got the most points for in the crowd that I ran with. Now, there were other crowds, where volleyball was number one. I was on the fringes of that. I knew how to play volleyball but I didn't play anywhere near as well as the kids who *lived* down in Santa Monica; volleyball was their number one thing. So there was body-surfing; there was volleyball. No board surfing--it hadn't been invented yet. That was a Hawaii thing. There were surf mats at that time, and a surf mat was, you know, you take the wave and you ride on this blown-up mat. Well, surf mats were totally *out*. You did not *ever* get seen anywhere near a surf mat because that was wimpy.

Ah, body-surfing. A big swell would come in, and you had to be in the right place, your timing had to be right. As the swell came, if you were just in the right place and you took about four strokes, real hard, you'd get your body moving as fast as the swell and then it would break with you. And you would slide down the front of the wave into the white water and it would carry you some distance. The people who could go the farthest on the white water before it finally dropped were the kings of the beach. Great fun. Because the waves in Santa Monica are always very consistent. They're not like the waves in the

Atlantic. The Atlantic is either a lake, with no waves, or it gets terribly rough. Once in a while it's in between, just right for body-surfing. And I've been to the Atlantic enough times to catch a few and it's great. But in Santa Monica, the bottom of the ocean slopes very gradually and so the waves come in in very good form. The shape of the waves is just right for body-surfing. Plus, there's a good space between the waves. They don't tumble over one another. It's not rough like the Atlantic. And so you get these big waves coming in one after the other with good spaces in bewteen them and they're just perfect.

How did you learn body-surfing? You watched the older kids. At first you got swamped by waves! I certainly did. But you watched the older kids and then you took your place in line--now, there's lots of people body-surfing down there. And everybody knows just where to stand. So what happens is, there'll be nobody, or just a few little kids playing in the water close to the shore and nobody out, and then there'll be a crowd of people right in the place where the waves break, and they'll all line up in a line, six feet away from one another, and here comes the wave and you'll see everybody paddling at once. Oh, gee, a wave can be long, all the way down the beach. Dozens, a hundred people trying to ride one wave. Like I said, you space yourself about six feet apart so you don't bump into each other. When it gets real crowded you're somewhat closer together, which means there's some bumping into one another and some growling and like that. At any rate, you all take the wave, and the question was, *Who* could go the farthest? Ron: he could always go the farthest. Ron-- and I'm jumping ahead a little bit, this was in high school--Ron was a poor kid, he slept in his car, an old beat-up car--but he was the most superb natural athlete. He high jumped six feet, and this was before the style of the backwards jump--he high jumped six feet in any old style! And somehow, no matter how perfectly you rode the wave, Ron would always ride it ten feet farther.

So, body-surfing was number one. Number two was, of course, girl watching and girl finding and girl getting. And there you had ten thousand different ploys for how you would see some girl on a blanket and somehow introduce yourself, including tripping and falling onto her. I wasn't terribly *adept* at using these little con businesses. I was kind of hesitant, I needed an introduction or some kind of a formal method.

MYRA: Or some woman like me who stood up and said, *"I'm going for a walk! Anyone want to come along?"*

ROGER: Let's put it this way. There were lots of guys who were better at getting girls than I was. I had a good reputation in the area as being a swinging dude, a good catch, so that I probably could have done much better than I did. But I was a little more hesitant than some of the other guys. On the other hand, my best buddy Mel had no inhibitions whatsoever. He was far and away the best girl-getter of the crowd. He was simply a *superb* girl-getter. He was also the toughest--that is, he was the best fighter. Without question, Mel was the charismatic leader of our group. And I was his sidekick. He was Lone Ranger and I was Tonto. He was Red Rider and I was Little Beaver. Well, you have to know the old comic books. Okay, that was number two. Body-surfing, then girl getting.

And then *volleyball*. Since we lived inland and didn't get to the beach that often, we couldn't compete with the Santa Monica beach rats who were down there every single day playing volleyball, and they were so much better than we were that we couldn't compete against them. So, we would play in little, wimpy volleyball games, but we didn't compete with big-time volleyball. But volleyball was also good. Now, the third thing was gambling. Okay? Crap games. Craps; that was a really big deal. As far as the game was concerned, the undisputed, number one leader was a kid named Stan. Stan is now a multimillionaire in real estate in Los Angeles. His home was in *House Beautiful,* he's in *Who's Who,* he's in *People* magazine, he is a very big man in L.A.

Stan was also a poor kid, from a divorced family, and again, in those days a divorced family was kind of a "whoa!" thing. But he was very much in there; he was one of the boys, no question about it. And as far as deals, wheeling and dealing, Stan was number one. There were some others that were in there with him. But the thing that Stan was the best at was gambling. Stan knew how to pad the dice. When you played dice on the beach, you played on a blanket or a towel. And you rolled the dice on the blanket. Now, if you could pick up the dice, okay, with only sevens showing--there's a way--and then you *roll* them so that the dice roll in this one direction and don't just tumble over each other, okay, your odds of picking up a seven were much greater than if you were in Las Vegas, where you throw the dice against a backboard and they bounce off like crazy! Stan knew how to throw the dice that way. Also, Stan always had money. There was a wonderful movie years and years ago with Gregory Peck and Lauren Bacall, called *Designing Woman*. In that movie there was a whole lot of hanky panky with gangsters. At one point an information man came up to Gregory Peck and wanted to sell him some information. He asked for a certain amount of money, and he always asked for the money by the name of the President on the bill, and he says, I would like a Grover Cleveland for this one. I think that's a five hundred dollar bill. At any rate, Gregory Peck says to him, "I don't have that kind of money; I'm not poor enough to carry that kind of money." The point is that Stan was poor enough to carry that kind of money. All right?

So. The gambling went on in little knots of people. The California beaches are enormously broad: they're almost half a mile. They're artificial, huge, and flat. Consequently, if you go way down near the water and have your game there, if any cops come to break up your game, you can spot them literally half a mile off, okay? And everyone can grab their money and disperse before the cops get down there. We used to see this happen all time; you'd see the police coming and you'd see people scatter. There was always a little knot of people; you could always see where the game was, because there'd be a knot of people. Nowadays, they'd be passing a joint around. There'd be people playing and everyone standing around watching it. Stan was always right there in the middle. Interestingly, after Stan made a bundle in real estate, he--what was that board game? Backgammon! Remember when backgammon became a big craze, about fifteen or twenty years ago? Stan financed a backgammon club up in the hills of Los Angeles. Okay? He was the backgammon *king* of L.A. Just carrying on!

People don't change, you know what I mean? They don't change. Stan was quite, *quite* a neat guy. Another thing Stan was very good at was girlies. Girls. Stan was not hesitant about approaching a girl, giving a girl a a line; he was very good at that. Consequently, some of the girls--well, *many* of us envied Stan his girls, okay? He had a *lot* of girls running around him. Gambling, girls, the whole business. You get the picture? He's a wheeler-dealer, but he's a good wheeler-dealer, not a dumb wheeler-dealer.

We knew some great people. Hey, I'll escalate the issue, okay? Next step up. Nice, quiet, mild mannered guy, not in my crowd--he was in a different club. He was in the Barons. But a guy that everybody liked, who practiced his trumpet a lot. He had a little band, and they played for weddings and bar mitzvahs and things like that. And I was interested in music. He knew my name and I knew his, and we talked to each other once in a while and met at social occasions from time to time; he was in my class and everything. *Herb Alpert*. We used to listen to "Mambo Del Crow" together. Herb Alpert was on the gym team and he was a ring man. He had a marvelous upper body.

MYRA: Let me tell you, his *face* wasn't bad either. We went to a going-away party for him the very first week that I met Roger.

ROGER: Yeah, he was a nice-looking guy and he had a good build because he was a ring man--

MYRA: *Very handsome.*

ROGER: One of his buddies from his club, the Barons, was named Larry Moss. Larry was a sidehorse man and I think also a ring man, also had a good build and all that. When they got out of school and Herb had finally found his sound, the Tijuana Brass, and his music started going, they formed A & M Records--Alpert and Moss, get it? Herb's family had some apartment houses; he had a background in business and he knew that you didn't let other people make money on you, okay? So when he had a hit record, instead of just taking a commission, he formed his own record distributing company. And had forty million dollars before the age of thirty.

MYRA: When Roger was in graduate school, he was at USC, and I had a part-time job working in the education department. And so Roger and I went to work together, kind of. I worked in the department of secondary education and one day some guy came in from a foundation; he was with the Herb Alpert Foundation! It was such a strange feeling, we were struggling along with these two kids while Roger was in graduate school, and here was the Herb Alpert *Foundation*. Sure, it was pretty weird.

ROGER: There was one other person that went to Fairfax High School and was in my class, and he happened to be the quarterback of the football team. He went on to be All-American and then played quarterback for the Buffalo Bills. His name is Jack Kemp: now, of course, a famous politician who just served as Bob Dole's running mate! Back then, Jack was in the Hi-Y, the club for Gentiles.

You have to understand that Fairfax High was about 95 percent Jewish. It was located in the very heart of the Borscht Belt in Los Angeles, which has Fairfax Avenue running right straight through it. And Fairfax High School is right at Fairfax and Melrose. This was the transition area for upwardly mobile Jews in Los Angeles. The bottom was Boyle Heights, which was located downtown. Very poor area, very tough guys. We had ties to those kids through other Jewish families. In fact, we even had a rumble with them one time, a fight. It's fortunate that the rumble never happened because *they* came with guns, knives, boards with nails in them, bicycle chains, and *we* came with fists. Had we ever gotten together, we would have been destroyed. The cops got there before we did, and they broke it up. They were genuine tough kids. We were middle-class. We liked to think of ourselves as tough kids. Okay? No way. Forget-it-city.

Now, the third end of that transition belt, from Boyle Heights to Fairfax, was Beverly Hills. When you made it, you moved to Beverly Hills, and that's where all the rich Jews lived, and they all went to Beverly Hills High School. Beverly Hills High School was an interesting contrast. In sports, they were a joke, with one exception. Tennis. They blew everyone away in tennis! And, yes, golf--but in football? Forget it. Those rich kids couldn't win football games.

MYRA: Well, of course not; their parents wouldn't let them play!

ROGER: But, on the other hand, they had connections. They were wealthy and everybody envied them. And consequently that was the direction that everyone was heading for from Fairfax High School. This combination of a mostly Jewish student body in a middle-class transition area, with Boyle Heights pushing from one end and Beverly Hills beckoning from the other--the academic pressure was so great that it became like the East Coast. Now, the East Coast and the West Coast are enormously different as far as academics are concerned. The East Coast is vastly more academically conscious than the West Coast. But Fairfax High School was an anomaly in that the pressure to make it, to achieve, to go to college, to be something--and the Jewish scholarship tradition--that was one *terrific* academic high school.

I had the best of both worlds in my youth. I had this bunch of guys who were fast and crazy and streetwise and all of that sort of thing who I ran with. On the other hand, I had this terrific high school that pushed me in math and chemistry. At one time when I was at Fairfax, we had the highest percentage rate of kids going on to college of any high school in the United States! It was a unique place. Well, I was mentioning Jack Kemp. There was a small group of *goyim,* non-Jews, at Fairfax, and yet I had no connection to those guys. Contrary to the old wheeze "Some of my best friends are Jewish," *all* of my best friends were Jewish. So, instead of joining the Hi-Y, which was the non-Jewish club where guys like Jack Kemp and I presumably belonged, I joined the Cardinals, which was one of several Jewish clubs. Jack Kemp and Bob Bergdahl, who went on to play blocking back for UCLA--a terrific athlete and a great guy--we knew them, and they knew us, and we were all friends, but we had kind of a deal. They were kind of over *there,* and they ran with the non-Jewish girls, who were in Tri-Y. We were the Jewish crowd, except that *I* was in the Jewish crowd, y'see? And everybody thought that was very weird of me.

There was one girl who was my counterpart. Her name was Elena and she was a non-Jewish girl in one of the Jewish clubs. She was in the Tantras. Yes, there were the Tantras and there were the Donatellos. Those were the two top Jewish girls' clubs.

MYRA: I was in a top Jewish club at L.A. High, the Baronettes, which I quit. The girls in my club were distinguished by wearing more makeup than everyone else in the school put together.

ROGER: Myra--have you got that picture? You have got to bring out that picture. This is the funniest picture you will ever see in your whole life.

MYRA: It's in one of my high school albums downstairs. We all looked like we were about forty-five when we were sixteen. I remember one of my friends, Jennifer, looking into the mirror in gym one day and saying, "My ambition is to be a well-dressed matron."

ROGER: But back to Elena, the non-Jewish girl in the Tantras club. She was just terrific. But she was one semester ahead of me--an older woman. In hindsight, and considering all the events that went on in high school, it occurs to me that I had a shot at her.

MYRA: Now he's going to call her up!

ROGER: But somehow or other, the fact that she was an older woman and all of that, I just never got there. But she was my exact counterpoint. She was the

only non-Jewish girl in a Jewish club and I was the only non-Jewish guy in a
Jewish club. We were the ones who crossed those club lines. And we could do
that because, well, the West Coast is different from the East Coast.

MYRA: *Rog*--at L.A. High you didn't cross lines. L.A. High was not as
overwhemingly Jewish as Fairfax. With us, you were either in a Jewish club or
a Gentile club, period: no mixing.

ROGER: The point is that Jews at Fairfax High ran things. It's not like there
was an establishment they were locked out of. They *were* the establishment.
They were confident. And when you're confident, you don't have to have rules
and barriers and stuff. Hey, if one of these *goyim* wants to join our club it's
wonderful. If that's okay with him, it's okay with us. That was their attitude
and that was my attitude.

MYRA: Roger, there were separate country clubs! And everybody knew that!

ROGER: Oh, yes; but we all considered that just complete bullshit. Really.
    Now, finally, getting back to what all us guys together did at the beach. The
fourth thing was getting a perfect tan. If you read "Doonesbury," with Zonker
and his perfect tan, click! That's for real. You have superb weather for nine
months out of the year. The perfect tan actually came along *with* all the other
activities. You didn't have to work at it. Only *girls* would work at it. The girls
would lie down with their eye protectors and that sort of thing and get the
perfect tan, and they'd spend twenty minutes on one side and then turn over for
twenty minutes on the other side, like a waffle, or whatever. The point is that
they didn't do body-surfing. Girls weren't athletes in those days. That was
very unfortunate. There were no girl volleyball players, no girl surfers--there
were a couple, maybe, but they were really an anomaly, wow, something else!
The girls simply came to the beach to look beautiful and to attract the boys,
okay? Had we understood that at the time--we were so young--had we
understood that all you had to do was walk over to a group of girls sitting there
on a blanket and say, Hey, my name is so-and-so and I go to Such-and-Such
High School; who are you?, and Hi, and that would have been fine! That was
all you had to do! But, God, there was a hurdle there: there was a psychological
hurdle; it was so difficult to do that. And so we would think up ploys of how
we could possibly meet. You know?
    You went to the beach, you got tan, you did all those things, and if you got
lucky you found out where a party was going to be happening. Party-hopping
was a very big deal. If you found out where a party was you would go to that
party. Now, the music of that time, well, this was before the rock and roll and
the "Surfing Safari" and the Beach Boys. That was all later. First, there was
the normal commercial music: Patti Page, Teresa Brewer, Johnny Ray, Vaughn
Monroe, Frankie Lane--I mean, it was *pittsville*. All of the girls were into that

music, and *all* of the parties were put on by girls. Guys never put on a party.
Girls put on a party. And they would have record players and records and stuff
and those would be the records they'd play. The best records were the Mills
Brothers. There were some good ones, but there were some dumb ones, too.
The other kind of music that we had available to us was rhythm and blues. It
wasn't yet called rock and roll. It was all black. None of the "good" stations
would carry it. It was on the little dink stations way up at the top of the dial,
that were in four figures; 1390 or something like that on your dial. Well, there
was a guy in L.A., a disc jockey, called Hunter Hancock. *Everybody* called
him Hunter Handjob. Hahaha! Everybody, everybody.

MYRA: I didn't even know he existed. None of this was part of my world.

ROGER: The name of his program was "Harlem Matinee." Okay? It was on
at night--I don't know where "matinee" came in.   And he had a little
introduction that he said: "Swing to sweet, rock to roll and blues to boogie."
Rock and roll was in there, but, you see, rock and roll were black terms at that
time. And he played all the nifty black music with all the double-entendre lyrics
--"Big Long Sliding Thing," for example, trombone player.   "Baby Let Me
Bang Your Box," supposedly about a piano player. "Work with Me Annie."
"Sixty Minute Man," later used in the movie *Bull Durham*. All of that good,
horny music. And of course what happened was that the genius of Elvis Presley
was that he took all that black double-entendre sexy rock music, rhythm and
blues, and he brought it into the white music system. Only with white musicians
playing would it be acceptable, dig? Yet you know how they used to call him
Elvis the Pelvis and all that business? He still managed to take that music and
make it okay for the white disc jockeys and that was the start of rock and roll.
It was the white southerners--Buddy Holly was part of that--because the
southerners were exposed to black culture. And all of these black musicians who
had pioneered all of that stuff, they lost millions when the white guys came in
and it proliferated for white audiences.
   But that happened just after I got out of high school and went to college.
Once I got to college, I was into studies, and I was out of the scene. And that's
when surfboards came in, and "Surfing Safari" and all like that, and what
happened was that all the things that us kids were *doing* when I was a kid
became commercialized. In other words, this was a way to sell products. It
became part of the national culture, the media culture. But we were there first.
   In my day, by the time you got to high school you were fourteen-- and
remember, you could *drive* when you were fourteen. *Lots* of us had cars when
we were fourteen. What you would do after that time is you would *drive* to the
beach, preferably picking up a couple of girls along the way, and you would
hang around and do your thing and get a tan, make your connections, whatever,
and get your evening set up. Saturday day, on the beach. Saturday night would
flow from that. Either you'd go to a party that you'd found out about on the

you'd put it on for the winter, or for the evening, and you would take it off for the daytime. And it was thick! It wasn't just one piece of canvas. It was multilayers of canvas with insulation in between. It really looked great. So, pleated and rolled upholstery, Carson top, skirts on the back--oh, and the *paint* job--

MYRA: Can you see how fascinating he was to me, this incredible creature, when I found him?

ROGER: Lacquer! Enamel was déclassé, it was the kind of paint they put on cars in the factories. You put on lacquer paint jobs, seventeen coats. The first several coats were just a base paint. The next few coats were metallic, metallic dark green, metallic dark blue, metallic *maroon*. Okay, then the last five or six coats were pure lacquer, so that it had *depth*. You would look *into* it. Looking into one of those paint jobs was like looking toward the bottom of a swimming pool, only on the bottom of the swimming pool there was all the treasure in the world shining up; that was the metallica shining out from underneath. And then you would drive down Hollywood Boulevard. And if you were really cool you would buy two different mufflers for your twin pipes. If you were supercool, you would buy two different mufflers, so that one would go [low pitch] balum, balum, balum, and the other would go [high pitch] balum, balum, balum, and the two together would make a *melodic* balum, balum, balum! It was super. And there was *one* muffler manufacturer, too; I can't remember the name, but there was only one--like Carson tops.

Now. Dark glasses, pair of socks, argyle socks this big, tiny argyle socks knitted by your girlfriend. Had to be a girlfriend; you didn't buy 'em in a store. A girlfriend knitted them for you, these little socks, hanging from your rear-view mirror.

MYRA: And a necker's knob on the steering wheel.

ROGER: Yeah, your steering wheel was covered with a a band of leather that was hand-sewn on the inside and it would have a knob attached to it called a necker's knob. And the necker's knob was so that you could drive with your arm around your girlfriend and you could completely steer at the same time. You always had a floor shift and you would teach your girlfriend to shift for you. That way you could sit there and drive with one hand on the necker's knob and one hand around your girlfriend and as you had to shift you would work the floor pedals and your girlfriend would shift for you, you see. Like that. Dark glasses, hair cut at the Blue & Gold, a flattop haircut, or--if you didn't get a flattop--a flattop haircut was generally for the summer and in the winter you would let it grow long and then it would be a big pompadour with a ducktail in the back. Levi's--rivet, button-fly Levi's. No zip fly! I don't know *who* ever bought those. Levi's. If you needed a jacket, a leather jacket. If you didn't need a jacket, a T-shirt. But a T-shirt that fitted right! Not like *this* dumb T-shirt. And if you did happen to buy a T-shirt that was the wrong type, you would take it and you would roll it up so it came just to the bottom of the deltoid. If it came up too high on the deltoid, that was déclassé: that was what the junior high school kids did. If it came down too low, that was no good. If it came just to the bottom of the deltoid, you could see the round of your shoulder; this would cross just under that muscle, and that was style.

And then you were cool.

MYRA: Now, I was familiar with a lot of this, but basically, I was looking to get good grades and doing what my parents wanted me to do, very active in school government; I was earning all kinds of awards, student body offices. I mean, Roger and I were like Mars and Venus.

ROGER: Postmortem. In 1978 we went on a vacation, the whole family, returning to California when the kids were fourteen and seventeen, and at one time we found ourselves passing through Santa Rosa. Santa Rosa is a medium-sized town up above San Francisco and inland. We arrived there in the early evening, and it was Friday night, and we were all tired and everyone was hungry. So after finding a motel for the family, Myra and I went out for doughnuts. And Myra and I drive into this doughnut place and we go in and we look around and both of us kind of look at each other, because *the scene is familiar*. There were all these *cars*. We see these custom cars, these hot rods!

MYRA: Kids driving in and out.

ROGER: There were all these kids, driving in and out and looking for each other. And we looked at each other and said--this is Friday night--this is like Hollywood Boulevard! This is cruising night! They've got all the cars and stuff from twenty years ago! And I said to Myra, "Let's go cruising."

MYRA: It was *so much fun*.

ROGER: And it was so much fun! We went down the main drag of Santa Rosa and it was bumper to bumper. In all the cars, everybody was playing the radio and they all had their radios tuned to the same station, so that you heard the same station everywhere. The kids were jumping out of their cars and jumping into other cars in the traffic jams, and the cops were all down the side streets. Mostly the kids were just talking back and forth and playing their radios. Talking back and forth, yelling "Hey, So-and-So," you know, and someone would jump out of a car and run down there. We'd drive by the side streets and we'd see the police cars waiting down the side streets because they *knew* that sooner or later there was going to be trouble. Because the problem is, when you go cruising, there's three kinds of people. There are people with dates who are cruising either before they go to a movie or after they get out of a movie and go to a drive-in. Just for fun, to show off that they have dates. There are people without dates who are looking for other girls and girls that are looking for other guys, people who are cruising for one another. But the third group are people who are kind of pissed off that they don't have a date or something like that and they're looking for a rumble. Aggressive people. Now, you get enough people out on Friday night looking for a rumble and they're going to find each other. And there's going to be a rumble.

The cops, of course, know this from long experience. They just wait on the side streets and let the parade go on, and then when there's trouble they're right on the spot. And that's how that fight that I told you about was prevented. For which I am eternally grateful. Remember how I told you that we almost had a fight with the Boyle Heights guys one time? It was prearranged, and they came with guns and knives and chains, and we came with fists? And the cops got there first? Like I said, I would have had my features rearranged, had we ever met, and I'm glad we didn't. Because we were naive, middle-class kids, picking a fight with tough poor kids. We didn't know how dumb that was at the time; we thought we were very cool.

MYRA: You know, there are laws against cruising in north central California now. Allegedly, it's a traffic hazard.

ROGER: Well, we had a ball; we cruised all the way through Santa Rosa.

MYRA: So Roger and I parked the car in the back of the motel and we were necking, we were in the mood, after watching all the cruisers; we had a wonderful time.

ROGER: It was super. It was high summer, beautiful, Friday night--and the cars were from twenty years ago, with their engines exposed! That's from when we were growing up in Los Angeles, and this was in Santa Rosa!

Now I'll finally get back to talking about parties, the point being that during my adolescence in L.A. we used to go cruising to see if we could find out about any parties. At parties, there were, again, three different activities that went on. There were boy/girl activities. There was eating and drinking. And there was fighting. Those were the things you did at parties. Unfortunately for the poor girls, the poor, poor girls who had these parties, the parties would always get out of hand. People would wait until their parents were out of town or something and then they would put on a party, and they would *invite* some people, but the word would get around and ten thousand people would come-- not the twenty that were invited. And the poor girls who were holding the party couldn't handle the situation; there was a great deal of destruction going on. I was moderately conscientious, taking into consideration the people that I ran with, and it always bothered me that there was so much destruction of property at these parties. *Rarely* would parties be held at the same place twice! Stuff spilled on rugs, and furniture damaged--so many rambunctious people and all. But, sometimes it would happen that the guys that were part of the crowd that was actually invited would take offense at the guys who were not invited to the party but just happened to show up, and ask them to leave. And of course this was the Signal, capital <u>S</u>, neon lights, okay. "Well! Why don't we just step outside [nasty laugh], all right? And we'll just settle this thing!" You see, that was great fun.

MYRA: But you were not a fighter, Rog.

ROGER: No, I was not a fighter. I traveled with fighters. I was involved on the periphery of fights but I was not a fighter. I didn't enjoy fighting. I enjoyed the fun of being where the fights were. But I was not a fighter. So other people fought and I watched, is essentially what happened. My friends would fight and I would be there.

Okay, party story. *Long* party story. This story starts while we are in high school, about tenth grade. We're hanging out, the whole Cardinals club is hanging, and we say, "Let's go out and have a war at the haunted house." The haunted house was a deserted military academy out in the valley. It was at the end of a long valley with hills around the back and the military academy kind of sat up a little bit on the hills; it was all boarded up and like that. A war meant, we would all get our BB guns; we all had BB guns, and we all lived close enough to the Mexican border so that we all had firecrackers. Firecrackers were illegal in California, but we could get them from Mexico. Ladyfingers were the smallest firecrackers. They were about an inch long and maybe an eighth of an inch in diameter, and they made a little "pop!" But they were genuine firecrackers, and the interesting thing was that they were the exact size of the hole in a BB gun. So. A BB gun runs on compressed air. No BBs; we weren't dumb enough to shoot BBs at one another in the dark. What you do is you take a ladyfinger, stick it in the muzzle of the BB gun, and light it and shoot it at somebody and it would wooshh, Pop! You see? And you'd have your own explosion. And these ladyfingers--I mean, obviously if they hit you right in the eye and exploded they could do some damage; but otherwise, no damage. A pretty good flash, not very accurate. You'd see the fuse burning, and then Foom, and it was fun. So, we would choose up sides, and one would go to one side and one to the other and fool around. And I had a BB pistol. I was one of the elite. I don't know where I got it but most people had BB guns, Daisy rifles they were called, and I had a BB pistol. The pistol was much easier to load because you didn't have to reach to the end of it, and it was really neat.

Anyway, so, we were up there, and we're playing our game, and we see the police. It was evening, night, and we see the line of police cars, because remember we were up on a hill and there's one road. Word goes out: *The cops are coming.* So everybody that was dumb ran to their cars and that was, of course, where the cops caught them. I was not dumb, and neither was a friend of mine, and we ran up into the hills in back of the place and hid in the bushes. So, after everybody had been caught, and, incidentally, all the cars were gone, and we were way out in the middle of nowhere--I had come with another guy--then we had to hitchhike home. Fifteen miles back into town. We made it. But what we did was we left our BB guns up in the bushes; we stashed the BB guns. Because we figured trying to hitchhike home with a couple of *guns,* we weren't gonna make it.

So. Next weekend I drove out to get my BB gun. And I got it, and I drove back into town and I ran into some friends of mine, who said, "Hey, there's a terrific party! Can we get a ride with you?" I said, "Okay, pile on." Well, it turned out that so many people piled on--I had people on the running boards, I had people in the rumble seat, I had about ten people on my '34 Ford, which was built for two--and we drive up to the party. Unfortunately, as we drove into the party, the police were already there. So, I tried to turn around. No way. The cops got us. They said, "Okay, what's happening? Everybody out; driver, show your driver's license," and then they searched the car. They searched the car and they came up with the BB gun.

And they said "Have you ever been arrested?" And so, honest Roger, I said, "Well, I've been *arrested,* but I've never been convicted of anything. Never even booked!" They said, "What were you arrested for?" I said, "Gang activity." Truthfully, that was associated with the rumble in Boyle Heights. So the cop looks at me and says, "Still at it, hah?" And once they'd searched my car, and found my BB pistol, they said "Aha! You're the one!" I said, "I'm the one what?" They said, "You're the one that's been shooting out all the street lights!" I said, "No way! Not me!" They said, "You're the one, and we're taking you down to the police station."

I yelled to a friend of mine, Al Chester, "*Al!* They're taking me down to the police station. If you can find someone else with a car, drive my car to the police station and park it out front someplace nearby so I can get home. And then have somebody take you back. Will you do that for me?" And Al said, "Sure." So I thought, "Cool. No sweat." I was not perturbed a bit. They drove me to the police station and they said, "Okay, tell us your story about how you shoot out all the street lights." And I said, "Number one, I don't shoot out street lights, and, number two, this BB pistol is not powerful enough to shoot out a street light. Furthermore, I can prove it." I was kind of a smart guy by then--this was high school--and I said, "What I want you to do is just take a piece of paper and hold it up. I've got BBs in my BB gun now, and I'll shoot the paper. If the BB goes through the paper, you've got me. All right? Fair enough?" They went along with it! They were *so dumb!* They didn't understand that you've got to hold the paper tight, otherwise the BB just pushes the paper aside. They held it up, I did my test, and of course, the BB didn't go through the paper! They said "Okay, okay; I guess you can go." I said, "Yeah;

thanks a *lot* for taking me down to the police station." So I walk out of the police station, feeling like a real smartass, look around--no car. No car. I was all the way at the Hollywood police station--I lived in West Los Angeles--and it was late at night, no buses running. Finally I walked all the way home. Ten miles, maybe twelve. *Long* walk. I got home and boy, I was pissed off. Next morning I called Al. "Where's my car?" He said, "It's right in front of the police station!" I said "Al, which police station?" He said, "The Pico police station." I said, "Oh, shit. They took me to the Hollywood police station. Okay, Al. Fair enough. It was an honest mistake." I walked to the Pico police station and sure enough, the car was parked directly in front of the police station --with a big ticket on it. My youth!

MYRA: One of the first dates that I had with Roger after we had started UCLA was as lookouts for a crap game. It was in my neighborhood, actually. My mother said, "Where are you going tonight?" And I said, "Roger's going to be lookout for a crap game and I'm going with him." She said, "All right! I'll make you sandwiches! In case they come and arrest you!"

ROGER: And we sat and necked while they played. See, I never had the money that these guys had. A lot of guys in the crowd traveled with a lot of money in their pockets. Fifty, a hundred dollars. And these were high school kids. They worked at various jobs and stuff. The idea of having a real honest-to-God *bankroll* in their pockets was a thing with them.

But let me say this. With us--with the Cardinals--there was a lot of little nuisancy gang activity, but no real crime. We didn't steal cars. I felt very safe. You know, you never even locked your car or anything.

2

Myra

Myra is a first-generation American on her mother's side, and as a child lived in a multigenerational, partially immigrant household with her reproving grandmother, who spoke little English. The constant reminder of Jewish emigré heritage, social boundaries and tribal loyalties haunted Myra as she moved through the aggressively all-American culture of 1950s California. She spent much of her adolescence emotionally divided between deep love for her family and strong attraction to the surrounding Gentile mainstream.

In high school, Myra joined a top Jewish girls' club, the L.A. High Baronettes, serving as club vice president; but unlike most other club members she also excelled academically and was a high officer of the Girls' Senior Board as well. As a socially active student government leader, Myra was known and liked by a broad range of people at L.A. High, her yearbooks overflowing with affectionate remarks from male and female peers and teachers. Yet Myra herself began to question the primacy of the whole club scene during her senior year, influenced by her more daring friend Sue. The combined attraction to Gentile boys and to a more "swinging" way of life culminated in Myra's relationship with non-Jewish Roger. While many of her Jewish girlfriends questioned Myra's decision to marry a Gentile, no one felt surprise that Myra won over the man she loved: her success with boys was well known.

Myra's internal discomfort with having a Jewish identity in a Jew-distrusting world affected much of her high school experience. This interview began in our family room one summer evening.

I brought the pictures up, just to show you where I'm coming from. Roger's been telling you the whole history of cool. But me, I looked like I was forty-five when I was fifteen. The whole point was to look older, in my club.

I ended up in the Baronettes. I remember my mother and sister encouraging me to join a club in high school. They gave me the impression that if I didn't join a club, I would probably regret it. I would feel out of it. So, I said okay, and called Rochelle and asked her for advice, and she said Baronettes. Years later, I heard a rumor that the reason I didn't get into the Dantes was because the Baronettes told them I wasn't coming back.

Before I pledged, see, I took this long trip with my family for six weeks in the middle of the school year. My parents decided to make a big trip east to visit my sister, who had just had her first baby. I went with them, *much against my will.* I was furious at having to miss all the social events, and absolutely *despairing* that I had to be away from Joe--a Gentile boy I loved--for six weeks! This was the worst torture that anyone could impose on me! In those days, back seats were nicely upholstered and kind of luxurious and there was a nice upholstered armrest. His picture sat next to me for the entire time. I talked to him, for crying out loud, for three thousand miles, and three thousand miles back. I was a fifteen-year-old girl!

Anyway--I didn't really belong in the Baronettes. Neither did Rochelle; maybe nobody belonged in that club! It wasn't so much the personalities. It was the collective appearance of all of us in the Baronettes. We obviously, collectively, used more eye makeup than the entire school, in fact several other campuses, altogether. You could not compete with us, until you got to Fairfax High School. There was a tremendous ethnic difference in the way people dressed, or looked, in high school, with some exceptions and crossovers. The Jewish girls wore all the makeup and dressed in that Hollywood style. And there were some of us who *swayed* back and forth and did a little bit of this and a little bit of that and crossed lines! I felt like sort of a Gentile Jew or a Jewish Gentile. Yeah, I did confuse people, with my chameleonlike personality. You know, a chameleon does that to protect itself, to give itself a protective coloring. And people like me who really want other people to like them--that's it, protective coloring all the way.

But the Baronettes, you've got the impression, *didn't* act differently at different times. Many really were shallow, pretty young women who seemed to have absolutely no interest in anything except dating. For instance, in the Baronettes was one of the prettiest girl on the campus, very striking, great figure, flamboyant clothes, and *lots* of makeup. I mean, mine is nothing.

Now, I didn't know her well. But she was really pretty and famous for her good looks. She never finished high school, but quit to be married in June. And the reason I mention her is because of a particular incident that struck me. We were all at her house for a club meeting shortly before she got married. She had a niece or a nephew there, an infant. And we were all going *eeewww* because this child obviously needed to have his diaper changed. And *she* was not about to change his diaper. And even then, as unliberated as I was, I remember thinking, She's getting married? She's quitting school to get married and here's this child, and she won't even change its diaper, and what is she going to do? Well, that was one of the Baronettes. But not all the club members were like that.

For our club activities, we had all of these elaborate rituals: scrolls that we would make for one another; teas--uccchhh. It was so absurd. The dressing up was a tremendous, expensive nuisance. But it was an important part of practicing to be our parents. Because that's what this was all about. We dressed up like our parents. We went to formal dances like our parents. We had *fundraisers* like our parents! We had rushing for sororities. Everything we did was a rehearsal for what we were going to do later: get married to someone of the right ethnic and social background. No other possibilities were discussed. We all knew what was expected of us. Education, possible careers, personal interests, talents, or opinions, or serious matters weren't important. The idea was to be prettty, popular, and cool. So we all bottled our serious thoughts and kept things *very light*. That's why I lapse into "airhead-speak" when I reminisce about that time.

To our club teas we would wear things like a suit. Women wore suits that were the equivalent of what somebody would wear to church. That's what you'd wear, a church type of outfit, with a hat. Everybody wore a hat! We all had hats, to go to these teas. And we're just fifteen, almost sixteen.

So. High heels. Gloves. Purse. Hat. All coordinated, of course. Then you arrive at the tea and the girls who were hostessing the tea were *really* dressed up. Now, Vogue--that was the top girls' club, the Gentile club--those girls wore formal dresses to their teas. I never understood the sense of this. Why would they have a tea in *ball gowns,* essentially? I thought that was very strange, but that's what they did.

Let me tell you about the two events of the year in each club. One was the Rush Tea, of which the vice president was in charge. And guess who got to be the vice president? Me. Of course. And it was like one hundred and fifty girls were invited. To somebody's house.

ROGER: You would make the perfect person to do the Rush Tea because you're very good at taking care of business and getting all the details done.

MYRA: Yes! Of course! I was practicing to be an adult when I did that. That's exactly it. Now, with the tea, everyone was responsible for making some of the food--or probably our *mothers* did it. People brought fruit salad and little sandwiches, and cookies. We had to have name tags, dishes, flower arrangements, and invitations printed; it was a whole big deal.

And then, in the spring, all the girls' clubs had dances. For dances, everybody had to decide on a theme, you know; it was pirates, or whatever. This other main event of the year was a semi-formal dance. There were two events. You'd wear a dress that was floor-length or ballerina-length and poofy and strapless. And the guy wore a suit. Guys didn't wear tuxes and they didn't rent dinner jackets; they just wore suits. And girls wore silver shoes and sequins. But formal meant evening wear. You either had to wear evening clothes, or, if you were either chintzy or independent, a guy could get away with a dark suit. And I guess we gave part of the money we collected to charity.

ROGER: They didn't sell tickets; they sold bids. They were called bids, right? Wasn't that right?

MYRA: No, bids were for being asked to join clubs.

ROGER: No! I remember! It was so peculiar to me that a ticket, which worked for every other kind of event where you had to buy your way in, was in this case called a *bid* for a ball. Crazy. It was all part of the extreme formality--

MYRA: *Charade--*

ROGER: I mean, the social pressure was *intense* that certain events be done in that particular way. And the way was, like Myra says, based on pretending to be an adult. To be a movie star, you know, or a celebrity.

MYRA: The social scene, as far as the events taking place, was run entirely by girls. The girls gave all the parties; some of the guys' clubs had dances. There may have been people at L.A. High who felt that the Dantes and the Baronettes were equal clubs, but to the girls that I knew, getting into the Dantes was numero uno. Baronettes was second. However, *boys* may not have felt the same way.

ROGER: I didn't get a sense of superiority. I just had the sense that there were these clubs, and there were some neat girls and some dopey girls in each club.

MYRA: When I started L.A. High, Vogue was like the Dantes; they were sister clubs and hung out together, although Vogue was Gentile and the Dantes were Jews. At first, the girls in Vogue seemed traditional, school service oriented, but not as academic a club as the Dantes.
   Vogue had club rings. We had club pins. And because I was vice president of the club--I was vice president of everything--I had all these other pins. Oh, God. Listen. When I was in twelfth grade--this is so *absurd.* And so embarassing, but I'm going to tell you.
   Every organization you belonged to, social clubs and school organizations, had a pin. So I had my Baronettes pin. And then in the twelfth grade I had a little gavel, because I was vice president; I refused the presidency later. So I had a pin with a little extra gavel. Then I was on the Senior Board, so I had my Senior Board pin. And I was Senior Board president. So I had my Senior Board gavel.
   Now, we've got two pins and two gavels. I wore this *every day,* to school. It was disgusting. *Totally* disgusting, that I would do this! But everybody else did the same thing.
   Except that I had about five different things I pinned on--I was like a *general.*

I had more pins than *anybody!* It was like the guys with their club jackets.

Well. I had a pin for everything I did at L.A. High, and the dopey thing was that we didn't have anything like a, a backpack or a *beanie* or something that you wore every day. No, every day you'd take all these pins off and the next morning you'd put them all back on! It took a long time!

The interesting thing about the clubs is that when we put on these events--it was such a tempest in a teapot to put on a tea!--anything that we did at school had a theme, and had colors, and then we had to order all the stuff that went with it. You ordered/made all the decorations. The table had to be decorated. And the flowers. Everybody worked really hard; if you were active in a club you worked hard. You were a community member. And of course we also had homework, sure. So if you were real active in school, or in school and sports, or school *and* sports *and* club, you were busy!

But the purpose of all the things we did was so--blah. *Supposedly,* we all did some charity work. But you should have heard everybody bitch about having to go put in their few hours a month at the children's hospital! Anyway, that's what the girls' clubs were like. But you realize that those of us who were active in all those organizations learned how to manage our time and responsibilities, how to get information, although most of this stuff was passed on from one president to the next. You didn't inherit a book or anything which would tell you your responsibilities, how to be in charge of this dance or that tea.

I didn't talk about sex with my friends. We told occasional tee-hee jokes that we'd heard. I really didn't know what my friends were doing. Nobody was that open about it. There was one girl who was "fast." Well, she wasn't in our club. This is all so stereotyped, but she was one of our friends who *wasn't* Jewish! She was a really nice girl, wholesome, probably much more wholesome than anybody else. And I remember the joke told about her was "Why is she like a doorknob? Because she gives everyone a turn." Yes. Terrible.

About sex: everybody wondered what everybody else was doing. That was the question of the hour. Was he or she doing it? And with whom? It was actually kind of amazing that anybody learned anything in high school, isn't it? We were so preoccupied. And oh, God--in junior high we had a special girls' assembly and the girls' vice-principal got up and talked to all of us about how we shouldn't wear boys' jackets. We weren't allowed to wear boys' jackets, so naturally, as soon as school was over, we'd put them on outside and walk home with them. And we weren't supposed to wear these pointy bras with "dividers." It happened that the style then was to wear sweaters and skirts, and you would decorate your sweater with pins, or a scarf around your neck--or something you wore on a chain. It became very popular to wear big, heavy medallions that hung down between your breasts, and a very pointy bra. And the vice-principal reamrked that we might attract boys by doing that, but what kind of boys would we attract? I don't think that the sermon was very successful. I don't think it altered *anybody's* behavior! But we didn't have those talks later, in high school.

However, I was such a true believer in high school that I was president of the girls' Senior Board--not so much because I believed that all those rules should be followed, but they were sort of there in place and I accepted them. And being girls' Senior Board president was the only way that I could be in cabinet class, the student officers' class, without having to deliver a speech to the entire student body, and that's the *only reason* I chose to be Senior Board president. Not because I was such a Gestapo person. In truth, though, my political convictions at this time were the worst. I remember some kind of interview that was in some paper, about how I believed we had to conform, that it was important to be a conformist. I can't believe that out of this set of beliefs and behaviors, at this point in my life, I met Roger. Can you imagine? We were coming from such totally different places.

ROGER: I knew the Baronettes. I knew they hung out at Agony Hollow. I knew who they were; I knew their *eye makeup*. And my general opinion was kind of like, That's an interesting phenomenon. Fascinating, what goes on down there with those girls. They're from somewhere else. They're different.

MYRA: Well, they were probably just like the girls at Fairfax.

ROGER: All right. My experience was that the Baronettes and the Fairfax Donatellos were very close cousins to one another. They were kind of on the same side of things. They were the same kind of girls, except that you guys were much more identifiable, specifically had a uniform, had a "look." It was the *Hollywood* look, with all the makeup on--to go on stage or on camera at any time. That was your look. Okay? You just have to look at your club picture! I found you kind of fascinating! Interesting! One had to have different ways of being, and different questions, and different attitudes, and a whole different outlook, in order to go out with one of *these* girls. And it just didn't occur to me to approach either the Baronettes or the Donatellos. Or the Tantras; they were more of the smart club, at Fairfax High. Well, all of these clubs had a range of girls. All of them had some nice girls--and some unbelievable girls. And then there was a crew of girls in the middle, who were socially very well-connected, did grand things internally in the club, and were always there, always organizing. They were the kind of club representatives who weren't very attractive, but they stayed at the very epitome of the social scene by being the *machers* of the school clubs. I knew those gals, and they were a real mixed bag, that group. Because some of them were insufferably parochial about their Goddamn clubs and school society, and it sounded like it was all written by the girls' vice-principal. They were beyond the pale. But there were others who were very open, and you're among their number. The smart girls, the alert girls, not the airheads. I was very friendly with them, and in fact even took out a couple. In fact I was asked out by *them*. It was really interesting. Ask a *goy* to dance! It was too much. Yeah, we were friendly. And that's exactly your slot, Myra, except you were *unusually* good-looking for a person who occupied this kind of nonbimbo role--

MYRA: You were either a saint or a slut! You had to be either a saint or a slut; there was little in between. Let me tell you, it was true.

ROGER: You were a *sensible* girl. Let's put it this way. Rather than an airhead, you were a person who knew something. You had thoughts. You were educated.

MYRA: The game, as I saw it, was to look sexy and behave like a saint. That was my compromise with my heredity, my family values, and my own inclinations. That's exactly what I did, you know, and that way I sort of pleased everybody a little bit. I got to please myself because I sort of pretended this whole image that was really racy. But I preserved my reputation and everything. I was, quote, a "good girl."
It's hard in our society. Everyone wants to be cool. I thought it was extremely cool of me, that I did both. In one way, I thought I was great, but in other ways I was extremely anxious all the way through high school. I did the same saint/slut thing with my schoolwork. I pretended to be a good student. I wasn't, really; I was a good parrot. I did exactly what was asked of me, not an inch more, as far as classwork. But I did everything beautifully, perfectly. I was very unimaginative. When I think about it, I shudder. Totally. I fed back what I was fed. And I got A's most of the time, when I tried at all. I had little real interest in what I was studying. I was interested in the people around me in the class, and in getting good grades. Well, I didn't get very much scope, in school. You didn't get much exposure to different things.
I also had fragmented loyalties. I had a very strong sense of loyalty to my family, and a desire to please them, which led to a very sharp conflict as I reached high school. It was easy, up until then, to please them. But the very first thing was that I fell in love with that first Gentile boy, Joe, which did not please my family at all, and I'm sure they were very relieved when he disappeared from the scene. I had this broken heart that I carried around all through the eleventh grade. But there came, after Joe, a string of crushes on Gentile boys. Always.
I liked the way they looked. That was it. You know? Opposites attract. It just happened that way. Also, a lot of things sort of converged when I got to high school; I had discovered boys a while back, but it became more of a *consuming interest* in high school. School activities interested me and I think a lot of that had to do with the fact that I became very good friends with Sue, who was in Vogue. It was the *top* Gentile girls' club. And so I had a toe in that door. Not a foot, but at least several toes. I went to a few events with Sue, and there were a couple of guys that I went out with. So unlike most of the girls in my club, who had only dated Jewish boys, I hung out with some of these kids.

Gradually, what happened as I went through high school was that Sue's influence overshadowed my club, so that finally I rejected the whole club thing in twelfth grade and dropped out. A lot of my good old friends were in the Baronettes, but my loyalties were being pulled in two directions. Sue was different, her background was different than mine. Sue, and the guys that she hung out with, and the things they did, were very exciting to me. What happened was I kind of stopped hanging out with my club. And they were absolutely furious at me, because having a student body officer was a feather in their caps. Their attitude was that now that I had "made it" I had turned my back on them. Which was true, in a sense.

I enjoyed the kids who were involved in school activities, and not many girls in my club participated. The club was *not me*. It *never* was. And I only joined it because I was convinced, by others, that if I didn't belong to a club I was going to be socially out of it. I don't think that would have been true, but I was scared to try, so I waited until I was a senior and then I dropped out. Yeah, that was kind of chicken. So I had *all* these different kinds of loyalties, and it was really strange. I didn't have all of my allegiance in any one place. But I will say this: I had a strong desire to please my parents. You know, I really had a divided life.

ROGER: There were also class issues. There were the other classes that we didn't see. The upper-class Gentile segment of society was absent, but Myra knew some of the upper-class Jews: the Beverly Hills crowd, the kids that went to Beverly Hills High School.

MYRA: There were relatives, and guys I dated, who had lots of money, and there were some connections to famous Hollywood people. For example, I worked briefly in Greer Garson's home in Bel Air as a secretary, and I went swimming at Danny Thomas's house. So, I sort of rubbed elbows--just a little--with much wealthier people. This was a very important goal for a lot of girls I knew, but I never cared very much. I felt that romantic love was so much more important!

But going to these kinds of events--dances, teas--it meant learning to put on the kind of events like you would if you became a Hadassah leader! It's true! And, you know, I can remember going to Las Vegas with my parents, going out with rich guys, and my parents getting a big kick out of it. They thought it was wonderful. Because, you know, I looked Hollywood. They thought I looked glamorous. The fact that they didn't mind that I looked sexy was--well, I knew very firmly that despite how I looked when I went out, I was supposed to keep my pants on and that was *it*. My mother made it very clear not only to me, but to Roger, that I was supposed to keep my pants on. Right? They had this scene on my eighteenth birthday--you never heard about that?

God, it was hilarious. Well, I had been going out with Roger for six or eight months. I met him in August, August 26, 1955. He was home on leave for a couple of weeks and then he went back to Fort Belvoir, and we wrote to each other for the next few months. He got out of the service just as I graduated from high school and I started UCLA a few days later; he was returning to UCLA too. We both started college in February 1956. Now, in May, my eighteenth birthday was coming up. And he had been kidding around for a couple of months, you know, that I was jail bait. He came to pick me up right after I turned eighteen. And he came to the door and said something, and as I'm going out the door he and my mother are *having it out* in the front hall. And I'm standing there, you know, like a *piece of meat*. And she's saying, essentially, "She better not," and he's saying, "Look, you had her for eighteen years; now I get my shot at her." And I'm standing there while they're debating my fate! Oy!

ROGER: I thought she had a lot of chutzpah to approach me on that subject. As far as I was concerned, that was a subject between you and your mother. I was not involved.

MYRA: Well, you know, I have to say that my mother, although she was often wrong, never lacked for courage. She didn't! That did take a lot of chutzpah for her to do that. I'm not saying she was right. She was anxious for my welfare and she was letting you know. She wanted you to keep your hands off me.

ROGER: I understood; I understood your mother. I understood where she was coming from. I knew all about that. And so I wasn't surprised or offended by her remarks. I just wasn't having any.

MYRA: We had two strong personalities who respected one another. And they were both having their say. It was kind of fascinating.

I remember one time when I was in junior high I went to a party that got out of hand. Everybody heard about the party, and people came from all over. I didn't go to those parties and I was kind of anxious; I was uncomfortable because things were getting broken. The place was getting kinda *wrecked*. And I called my mother to come pick me up; I wanted to get the hell out of there. Somebody was throwing up on the lawn; the bed was broken in one room; nobody was screwing, but people were jumping up and down on the bed. And the father was disabled and the mother was frightened; they wanted everyone to leave, but were kind of hiding in the kitchen.

And my mother came to pick me up and she took one look at what was happening. In the dining room, some kid was carving a candle into shavings all over the table. It absolutely infuriated her. She walked in, saw this ailing man and his terrified wife, and my mother, at her full four feet eleven inches, my mother said, "All right! This party's over. *Everyone's going home.*" And I mean she just stood there and cleared the place! My father was waiting in the

car. He didn't clear it up; my mother did! She was like that. She was tough.
She really was.

3

Pat

Pat is Roger's younger sister. Like Roger, she spent most of her childhood as a Hollywood film extra and print model and was often glamorized and overdressed for school by her ambitious mother. During high school, Pat left the Screen Extras Guild, but her beauty and presumed sophistication made her a much-sought-after club candidate. She pledged Vogue, the top Gentile girls' club at L.A. High, after rejecting bids from several other clubs.

Although Pat entered high school "knowing the game and how to play the game," she soon led two lives, regularly forsaking the wholesome club activities for more rebellious jaunts out on the town with a circle of girlfriends. Her testimony of *female* cruising, drinking, and nightclubhopping is a significant example of the ways young women did, in fact, challenge the behavior codes so strictly established for them. Pat's involvement with a subgroup of friends called "The Dirty Seven" led her to question and eventually abandon club guidelines; to engage in forbidden alliances with boys; and to make tentative forays into the surrounding black and Chicano communities.

Pat's high school years ended in early marriage, rather than in the college experience she had begun to envision. But as an older adult, she completed training and certification as a therapist and opened her own successful practice. She thus brings to her own past a unique combination of remembered raw material and contemporary professional perspectives on gender issues. This interview took place during an afternoon drive on that most breathtaking of all road trips, the stretch of Pacific Coast Highway winding south from San Francisco.

I was in high school from 1954 to 1957, right? Well, kiddo, the deal was, when you were still in junior high--when I was at John Burroughs--you were already primed for going into high school and being pledged. And the word was already out at my junior high about the best clubs to pledge. So by the time I got to high school I pretty well had the scoop.

You didn't get pledged in your freshman year; the freshman year was when you--God, there was a word for it. I want to say "ran," but that's not right--*rushed!* Yeah! So, the freshman year was when you rushed. And the high school had a policy--the school was trying to be fair or inclusive or something--that every single freshman girl had to be invited to all the appropriate freshman rushing activities. Depending on whether they were Christian or Jewish. There *were* people in between. One girl was certainly Jewish *and* otherwise. I'm not sure what the otherwise was. She was sort of this half-and-half person, and she ended up being a Vogue. And I have no idea how that happened to be. She must have identified more with her Christian side.

There were these separate clubs for Jews and white Christians; but blacks and Asians and Mexicans? They were treated as nonpeople. I think the school made a case for this shit--that they could belong to the school-sanctioned clubs, but basically *all* the clubs were school-sanctioned, including the social clubs--you know what I'm saying. They could, certainly, be part of the photography club. And *if* they were Christian, they technically were invited to the rush teas and dances. They were never excluded from the invitations, but none of them ever came. They *knew better.* There were times, I think, when one or more of them might have actually thought they were *really* being invited, you know, and went, but I don't remember any of them ever showing up. Everybody, I'm sure, would have been very polite, but it would have been, like, this very uncomfortable situation.

You rushed with people of your own background. And how they did that I have *no idea*--I mean, how they went through those lists of students and figured it out. Unless the administration did it, since they were part of it. Clearly they gave out the names, or they might have even made the lists, dividing up who was what. But the administration really didn't have anything to do with determining which club was "top." They just had to do with supplying the lists of students' names, indicating Jews and Gentiles.

All the clubs were required to invite all the girls in the freshman class, of either Christian or Jewish persuasion, to their rush teas. That was the up-front, legitimate thing. The deal was that some girls never went to all the teas. They only went to certain ones, or the ones that they thought that they wanted to get involved with. So, certainly, not all the girls showed up at all the teas, and that's interesting to me. The freshman year was about rushing and you went to these various formal teas and were invited to informal kinds of activities, and at the end of freshman year there was something called Bid Night. You got together with your friends and hopefuls. It was a big, special night. Why do I think the bids came in over the phone? I can't remember how it happened--whether the bids were all mailed out and everybody got them in the mail the same day--but it seems to me, if I remember correctly, that at the Bid Night party we were all sitting around not knowing for sure which bids we would get.

It was a slumber party, and people would call home, and find out that they had gotten a bid to a particular club, and everybody would scream and yell, and shit like that. Some girls would be waiting all night long, hoping that they were bid to the particular club they wanted. And if they didn't get that particular bid--ah!

I remember this intense excitement. There was this whole big group of girls that were together, hoping that they got bid to Vogue. The way it went for the Christian clubs was that the best Christian club was Vogue and the second-best was Cajun. There was a third one, and I can't remember the name of it. Then there were two Christian boys' clubs. I want to say Nobles. There were two, and one was better than the other. One had sort of all these football player type jocks in it, you know, the obviously jocked out, good-looking group; the other club had the scholarly, student body president types. Right. That was the deal with the boys' clubs.

Vogue had girls who were straight-A students and part of the Junior League and service clubs. Vogue also had some very wealthy girls. L.A. High encompassed two areas of old money. Now, a lot of those girls went to private schools, but the ones that didn't go to private schools were at L.A. High. I'm trying to remember the names of the two old neighborhoods. One was over off of Sixth Street and one was, God, this one with gates and shit over off Wilshire Boulevard. There were some girls invited into Vogue because of their social standing and because of their money. There were some girls that were invited into Vogue because they were good-looking, period. There were some girls that were invited into Vogue because they had great personalities. These were the criteria! You had to have either a really great personality or you had to be really good-looking or you had to have money and social standing. There were, maybe, a couple of girls that were in there because they were clearly *smart,* really bright. You had to have some combination of those things or be outstanding in any one of those things to get into Vogue.

I was at the slumber party and it seems like I called home and my mother said that I had received a bid to all *three* of the Christian girls' clubs. Rock and roll! They could all bid for you, or one or two could bid for you, and I got bids from all of them. It was very clear to me that if I got the bid from Vogue that that was the *one to do,* you know. You bet! That was the one.

Okay. So, we're at the end of freshman year, and we have received our bids, and we go into sophomore year. I don't remeber if there was a ritual about *accepting* your bid. But I do remember then you had to go through this pledging bullshit, the first couple weeks of sophomore year. I do remember being assigned a big sister, and my big sister was named Nancy House. She was a senior, a senior Vogue, and she wrote me this thing on a scroll made out of parchment paper that was burned around the edges, rolled up and tied with a ribbon, had some sort of artwork-type stuff on it.   You were supposed to do these things in a nice way. So, she was my big sister and she was supposed to help me and sort of *guide* me into all the rules and rituals of Vogue, of which there were many! Her job was to teach me and be my sort of *shepherd.*

The rules and rituals of Vogue? You had to subscribe to a particular code of ethics, or a moral code or a loyalty code, that you wouldn't disgrace the club. At all times engage in appropriate, feminine, graceful, good-mannered behavior. You could not behave in *any* sleazy way with guys. That was unclearly stated in writing, but what it actually meant was that if you were found out, if you were actually found to be fucking anybody, that was it. That was sleaze. That was unwritten, but even below that was if you had a steady boyfriend and you were fucking, the deal was nobody would say anything as long as you were cool about it. But if somehow somebody saw you, you were *out*. You were also out if you did any other kind of sleazy things like let guys feel you up in the bathroom where anybody else could see. So you basically had to keep your sexual behavior extremely private and act as if you weren't engaged in it, other than general making out, which was sort of frowned upon but you wouldn't get, here's a word, "blackballed."

So, anyway, your big sister would indoctrinate you into this particular code of ethics. You couldn't fail, or get kicked out of school, or do any sort of outrageously inappropriate rebellious behaviors. You had to agree to give so many hours per week as a Candy Striper, which was volunteering to go down to Children's Hospital and read to the sick children. There were other options, but that was the one I remember doing. Candy Stripers wore these sort of aprons, with pink and white candy stripes. You had to agree to be helpful and participate in the school dances. I think we paid some kind of dues, and that went toward the dances, which were big deals. There were other activities to gather money for the dances. So your big sister told you about all this stuff. You got to wear a ring. And it seems to me there was a pin. You could wear either or both.

But back to the beginning of sophomore year. Pledge Week. You had to walk around behind real club members and be attached to them. Anyone who asked you to be attached to them, you sort of had to walk several paces behind and do anything they told you to do, like buy their lunch or carry their books from class to class and other strange and slightly humiliating things--but nothing like eat raw liver or anything like that. The guys did that whole number. The girls basically did this you're-my-slave-for-the-day trip, and you got to do that for a week. That was Pledge Week, and you had to do that with a certain amount of grace, and not complain. Yeah, it was sort of "Down on your knees, pledge"; "Three steps behind me, pledge"; "I spilled my Coke, pledge, wipe it up with the hem of your dress": that type of trip. This was a week's worth of kind of being this doggy person. And at the end of Pledge Week, the little pledges got together--Oh! Right! They fucking had all the pledges in one room, right, in this big house, and the "real" members would be in another room in this big house and they did this ritual number.   They were supposed to be scaring you, you know, to let you know that you were still on trial. You weren't a real Vogue yet. But everyone knew that unless you really fucked up and told everyone to go to hell or something, that you'd be accepted. So there was this big ritual with them in one room and us in another being all twittery, and then one by one they'd call us in and get us to recite how to be a good Vogue, and that we knew what the requirements for being a good Vogue were, that we were grateful to be a good Vogue, you know, and then they would hand us our pins. Or our rings or something. We were then officially accepted into the main room and into the club. And that was the big deal, at the end of Pledge Week.

I will tell you this other, more personal stuff about Bid Night. On Bid Night you were hanging out with people you knew from junior high. We were still freshmen. You were hanging out with other freshman girls, some of whom you'd met that year and some of whom you'd known from junior high school and who were your buds. Right? And there was this horrible scene about--about who was being chosen. What if we both don't get chosen for what we want? What if you get chosen and I don't? And no one really talked about that. You know, people tried to save face and say, Oh, I really don't care which, it doesn't matter, but that was bullshit, because most people wanted a bid to Vogue. And there were some people there who were my friends who didn't get a bid to Vogue. And that was a very wildly uncomfortable thing, I remember, how it was like a ritual separation. It was bottom line, we knew that. No matter what we said in that room, on that night, we knew that if this person got a bid to Vogue and this person got a bid to Cajun, that was going to separate us. It's not that we wouldn't be friendly or say "Hi" in the halls or, even, occasionally, get together, but we're now in two separate deals. And there was kind of a strange acceptance of all that, that somehow these people who were deciding about us were deciding who was going to go into one cattleyard or another. And that would be it! Somebody else was going to say, *you* get to belong with these people and *you* get to belong with those people. That, in fact, is what happened. A bunch of teen-age girls decided who was good enough. I think their parents had a hand in it.   But it was sort of grade A meat, grade B meat--literally! That was sort of the stamp of this thing.

Well, it wasn't just all about looks, although that was certainly important. You could be a righteous *airhead* and if you had looks you could still make it into Vogue. Anyway. In the wings, somewhere, there were parents. I don't remember them very clearly, but there were parentlike advisers. They seemed to always be mothers of girls who lived in the big wealthy houses, of which I was not one. I don't know what they had to do with the choosing--I'll tell you why I'm vague on some of this. Like Myra, by the time I was a senior, I was no longer interested in any of this. And didn't really participate. I dropped out of Vogue when I was a senior and didn't participate in any of the choosing.

I was selected, I think, because I was a hot-looking babe and because I had a good personality--and because I was adept at playing the game. I knew, walking into high school, what the game was and how I needed to play it, and I was good at it. It never occurred to me until later in high school, toward the end of my junior and clearly all of my senior year, to question the unfairness of the whole scene.   Early on, it was just much more important for me to be part

of it, to be included and accepted as stamped grade A. I took for granted that
these divisions were going to be made--first, the Jews and the Christians in
different camps, and that seemed quite fair to me because we each had our own
clubs. What seemed strange, and which again I didn't question because that's
just the way it was, was that most of my friends from junior high, because I'd
gone to John Burroughs, were Jewish. And we already knew, automatically, in
junior high, that we were going to be in different social groups in high school.
We all just accepted it. We didn't question it, or say, "Oh, too bad," or "Oh,
this is weird," or "Who decided about *this?*"

It was like "Now you are more grown up and you have to be with your own
kind. You have to learn to date your own kind of people." And I think this was
equally supported by both the Jewish and the Christian families. "You want to
start figuring out how to find a nice Jewish boy and we'll give you the context
to do it; this is where you do it."

Mostly, we had teas. Oh, *God.* I *hated* the teas. Well, you know, the teas
were *white gloves.* And high heels. And inviting your mother. They were social
teas. I can't remember what, if any, importance they had, other than to teach
us how to be socially appropriate young women and to *sit around.* We made the
sandwiches, come to think of it; we did the work. We decorated the room, and
decoration was a big deal. We figured out little themes for the teas. Themes
were a big deal. We did the flower arrangements. Got ourselves all dressed up.
Had our mothers come. Basically, our mothers got to meet each other and chat.
And we were these lovely little social little women, who poured tea with our
fingers sort of up, and wore dresses and white gloves--I remember them because
they were so *weird*--and did ladies' small talk. It was this training thing. That's
why I think we had to have a certain number of rich girls in the club, because
they had the houses that had great big winding stairways and huge rooms and
libraries and gardens and pools, you know, and we had these teas in these grand
old estate homes.

We were pretending to be upper-class. We weren't all rich. But we were
pretending to be, having the teas in these places--this parody of upper-middle-
classness. Oh, I think my mother loved it. This was her great hope. I think she
was thrilled. But the teas were very strange for me.

There were teas, dances, and always the ritual of the new pledges, Pledge
Week and all that shit. We did a couple of dances a year, and dances always
included having to go around and get your *parents,* of course, to put ads in the
dance catalogues. Dances had these catalogues with advertising. They weren't
exactly dance cards. Little books, programs. And the dances, again, had these
themes! There were decorations, there were committees--there was a lot of
work. They were big deals. And you invited other clubs. I even remember that
we went to dances at other schools.   Some groups at Fairfax would put on a
dance, and they would issue an invitation to our club. Dances were big. Oh,
themes! Themes, oh, my God. Oh, they had these catchy little names. I don't
even know if I can get my mind in the space to do this. Oh, for instance, Spring

Fling. That, I'm sure, was the name of one of them. And we always had a summer dance.

I think a couple of things alienated me by my senior year. The people I ended up getting tight with, in Vogue, were all a year or two ahead of me. So I ended up not hanging out very much with my freshman class but I hung out with an older group of girls. And when they graduated and left it felt like I had lost my group. The other thing that happened was that I--this is more vague--I began, at some point in my junior year, to be aware of having a functioning mind. And it began to work. And I thought that the activities and the rules and the dress code shit were limiting and twitty and inconsequential and unimportant. It was one of the things at the time I rebelled against. It represented to me everything that my mother wanted me to be, and everything that I thought was going to limit the *shit* out of me.

Here was the dress code--or at least what we wore to school. Skirts and sweaters. Matching. Full skirts, straight skirts, matching sweater sets, that kind of stuff. We did get a talk about how to dress and how to behave like young ladies. And it was a lot about rules: your skirt had to be so many inches from the floor; what kinds of *socks* you had to wear. In high school you either had to wear hose with your flats or you had to wear bobby socks. And of course everybody who was cool at all never wore bobby socks with flats. You wore bobby socks rolled down twice with your white bucks, and you wore stockings with your flats. In junior high, there was the girls' vice-principal, who would give the girls these little talks about how to dress correctly, and how to behave yourself. In high school there was something called the Girls' League.

The Girls' League was this sort of bunch of smart girls. It was a service club. And the best that I could figure out was that they were like cops. They were girls' cops. And they would go around and watch for girls who were dressed inappropriately and write them out citations. I hated them! And I hated wearing stockings and oftentimes I would take them off in the middle of the day. And, you know, I had shaved legs and all that good stuff, but if one of *those girls* came along they'd *pinch your leg* if they were unsure that you had stockings on. Not hard. But especially if they were jealous of you. Especially if they were ugly girls they'd pinch you. If they thought you looked too sexy, they'd come along and they'd pinch your leg to see if you were wearing stockings or not. And if you weren't, they'd write you up with these stupid citations.

I hated them. I thought they were awful. I just fucking hated them, kiddo. Because they were my peers! And what right did they have to judge me and what I was wearing? Like, was my sweater too tight--oh, and *God forbid* if you didn't wear a *bra* on or something like that. *God forbid* if you were wearing a blouse made out of cotton, or nylon, whatever, that was sheer, and you could see your bra through the blouse.   *God forbid* if you were not wearing a whole slip with an upper part. You were not allowed to notice bras through anybody's clothes. That was part of the deal. If you had something on that you could see a bra through you'd *better* have a whole slip on. I'd forgotton about that. Yeah,

I didn't like the Girls' League.

There were also rules about makeup. Let's see if I can remember. You got to wear lipstick, but not in junior high. I think at that time eye makeup was just starting to come in, but the Vogues didn't wear much eye makeup. We were trying to be Debbie Reynolds.

I had been a movie kid, which was another aspect in my life until I was sixteen, and I put my foot down and said, "No more." So when I was a freshman and a sophomore and for part of my junior year I was still doing films. Until my sixteenth birthday. At that point there was a requirement with the Screen Extras Guild that you join the adult version of SAG when you turned sixteen. There was some fee, or a different fee--anyway, a transition period when you reached sixteen years old. I guess then they considered you were no longer a juvenile. And I said "No. I just don't want to do it anymore." I don't remember it being such a glamorous deal for me; I'm *really* aware that it was a big deal for other people. I personally was made so aware of the *lack* of glamour in the whole Hollywood scene, and the grossness of it all--you know, [a legendary Hollywood actor] feeling me up behind the fucking *props* when I was eleven years old. Oh, yeah, sure, that was part of the deal. Hollywood was not in the least bit glamorous to me, nor did I have any hankering for it, but there were certainly girls in the club who spent lots of time with nails and styles and makeup and stuff. It was not my thing. It was Myra's thing. But my bit parts in movies--I'm sure that was an incredible ticket of admission to Vogue. That was part of my *allure,* I'm sure.

People would do movie star gossip at me. That was never my thing. I recall that some of the girls were interested in Brigitte Bardot. Marilyn Monroe for sure, Brigitte Bardot might have been later. There were all these twinkletoes people like Doris Day and what other twinkletoes types--Sandra Dee. *Debbie Reynolds!* Take Doris Day and Debbie Reynolds and that was Vogue. Okay? If there were any role models that Vogue was going to be patterned after, it was that kind of blond bobby-socks-ness. The sweet girl next door who could certainly put on white gloves--and be glamorous without being too sexy, because sexy was dangerous and lower class. And, see, I think Myra's group might have had more emphasis on the glamorous part, but Vogue was more girl next door. Wholesome. You're talking blond wholesome. Debbie Reynolds is a perfect example. You know, not stupid, but sweet and kind, and sort of--*that.* *That* was the Vogue style. Certainly not Monroe or Bardot, but not even somebody who might have been a *bit* more glamorous. Or sophisticated. See, if *I* had a role model at that time it would have been Lauren Bacall.

Let me tell you how the moral shit came down. It was not explicit. No one sat down and said, "Hey, listen." It was couched in the most obscure terms, but we knew exactly where the limits were. The boys practiced more dealing with the world at large, because they were getting ready to go out into the world, and part of their dance was to have rumbles, which were fights, which were survival-of-the-fucking-fittest bullshit. And so one club from one school would stage some stupid fight with another club from another school and all the guys from all the clubs from all the schools would then get the word that there would be a rumble on such-and-such a night or Saturday morning or whatever and they'd all go out and fight. So they were preparing themselves for the world. And that's *how they prepared;* it's very interesting.

We prepared ourselves for the world by practicing being good, social, socially prudent, ignorant, limited *wives.* We had our little rituals about that, and we knew the guys went out and fought, and the deal was Friday night the guys tended to hang with the guys. And I guess they drank or catted around or whatever the fuck they did. And the girls hung with the girls or stayed home. The *good* girls stayed home on Friday night and went out with their special beau on Saturday night. That's when you showed up with the person you were going steady with. Part of my defection from that whole Vogue scene started late in my sophomore year, when I was barely initiated, and continued through my junior year until I started dropping out. You see, there was, within Vogue, a subgroup, and we called ourselves the Dirty Seven.

Totally cool. Totally cool. This is my favorite story, my favorite part of being a Vogue. The Dirty Seven stayed well within the realms of respectability. But we clearly, by virtue of our name, were faster than the others, okay, which meant that we could get away with occasionally cutting school in the afternoon and we'd get into somebody's car and go to Scrivner's and smoke cigarettes and drink coffee. Scrivner's was a drive-in about a mile from L.A. High. The Dirty Seven also went out cruising on Friday nights, and I was often the driver, and our deal was that we imitated the guys. We drove down Hollywood Boulevard, shouting out of the car window when we saw a good-looking group of guys, and they cat-called at us, and we cat-called right back. We drank beer. We never got drunk in public. We did all this, again, within the realm of respectability, but we were clearly on the edge. And we were good-looking enough and sharp enough and popular enough so that nobody really called us on it. We stayed on the edge. We were the Dirty Seven.

The deal with me--and it's very interesting looking back--I did not like drinking. And when the Dirty Seven went out they drank these little tiny cans of malt liquor. They were really small cans of malt liquor and it was supposed to have more alcohol in it than other kinds of beer. I can't remember what it was called; it's obviously not made anymore. But that was the cool thing for them to drink. I hated the taste of it. I thought any kind of alcohol was so gross. I remember the first time I got drunk. This was early in high school; I went to some party and it was on this punch that somebody had made, throwing in a whole bottle of--even the *words* make me ill to think of it--*sloe gin,* oh *fuck! Sloe gin*--it was not very slow! It was this syrupy, gross stuff like grenadine, right? You couldn't taste the booze, and so I drank a bunch of this punch. One of these jokes, ha ha. I got way sick all over the place. I did not like the taste of alcohol, so what I would buy while the other girls were buying this beer was Manischewitz loganberry wine. And it tasted good. You'd sip this Manischewitz loganberry wine and it was like Kool-Aid. The idea of it right *now* is kind of sickening to me, but it tasted good. And that was my drink.

I remember that. I remember every one of those girls. We used to hang around and we would listen to jazz. This was different from the rest of our peergirls who were listening to the sobby songs, I'll love you always, you'll never leave me, Patti Page and shit like that. It's not that we didn't know that, but we were also listening to people like Nellie Letcher and rhythm and blues that had dirty language in it and we saw ourselves as more sophisticated and worldly. The Dirty Seven group liked Julie London and her smoky voice and her bluesy singing. We were into her. We were not into Patti Page. That shifts us over into a totally different area. That was our idea of glamour. We were learning to drink and all of us smoked. We would swear, though certainly not in mixed company. We took risks, went to places and pretended to be twenty-one. We went to some blues clubs in East L.A. where black people went, and that was like *wow,* if our parents had found out!

We dressed up and went into those places and acted as if we were older, and listened to this music. That was like unacceptable. For us, the Dirty Seven, to go downtown to Central Los Angeles and scout out these clubs, where the majority of the patrons were black, for us to go in and sit there and listen to these great blues, was just the most baddest possible thing. Nobody there ever bothered us or disturbed us or was rude to us at all. It was kind of--different. There was this strange, stereotypical respect. Now we're in the black place and they're doing this great black music and we were like sort of these accepted guests. We knew that we needed to be very proper and respectful because they were doing their black thing and we weren't supposed to be there. It was like we were in territory that wasn't cool. And no one there would have *ever* made a pass at us. Nobody ever did, and we were pretty good-looking, got all dressed up and all duded out. So it was a whole different scene. This was *their* world. And it was *way* forbidden territory. And we did stuff like that, the Dirty Seven, and we were a fast, great group of women.

And the interesting thing about us, unlike the rest of the girls, is that men and boys were not central to our group. We would talk, sometimes, about our boyfriends, but it was not necessary in our particular group to have a steady guy; whereas, in the rest of Vogue, if you did not have a steady boyfriend who was on the football team or in the right whatever, that was kind of not okay. And that wasn't our trip. Jeannine--she was totally in love with this guy Bill and oftentimes would choose to be with him rather than to come along with us. And we used to razz her about that and get mad at her about that. We were this great group, this sort of offshoot, on-the-edge women who never came right out and *said* we're not really sure we want to do all this tea stuff, we want our lives to be more exciting. And when they graduated and left and I looked back at the other stuff that was still going on, there was no way I could relate to it. Or wanted to be any part of it.

I never turned in my pin. I just declined being active. And no one ever kicked

me out of the club. I did not ever make a formal protest. I just stopped going
to the dances, stopped being on committees. And nobody ever came after me
and said, "You can't be a Vogue anymore." Damn it, I eventually, down the
line, lost touch with every one of the Dirty Seven and it wasn't until about six
or eight months ago that I started wondering, really wondering, about what
happened to them. And I'm moving closer to the place where I'm willing to do
the footwork to look them up. Like Myra reconnected with Sue.

We were apolitical. There may have been a few girls in Vogue who were
more the academic types, who I didn't hang out with, who were on the debating
team. *We* were absolutely antiintellectual. To be an intellectual, a thinker, was
completely uncool. Other than getting good grades: it was good to get good
grades; it was important. But you didn't walk around being a thinker! That was
---if you were smart, it was about the classroom, it didn't have anything to do
with social stuff. And you didn't enter into or start or engage in any kind of
intelligent conversation at all, that I remember. Ever.

That was one of the things that happened to me when I was a junior. I got
into this class and I had this teacher. For the first time in my life ever, ever,
that I can remember, somebody actually treated me as if I had an idea, a brain.
And so this was an incredible awakening for me, that was also augmented by
Roger. That was part of what helped me disengage from the Vogues and all the
rest of the bullshit.

Roger was dating Myra at the time. He was interested in classical music. He
gave me Ayn Rand to read. He thought that Ayn Rand was just wonderful; Ayn
Rand was like this revolutionary, thought-provoking person in his life. And who
else--Orwell, those sort of visionary people. He started me out with Ayn Rand's
The Fountainhead, then Aldous Huxley. My God. It was a secret between Roger
and me. This was our secret, that I was reading these books. It was a secret
from my club-mates. This intelligent relationship that I was having with this
teacher, feeling spurred to write more and more important stuff about the books
he gave us to read in class--I don't remember what the course was--was also a
secret. This was not what I was being prepared for in my life by anybody.

Myra was actually in the same class with the girls that I hung out with. Myra
and I, we'd see each other, say hi, talk about Roger. By that time I was already
turned toward my more sophisticated phase. And already had for the first time
in my *life* a connection with my brother, who was taking me, the little sister,
along *with* Myra to jazz concerts and stuff like that. And that caused me to be
more loyal to Roger and Myra. Here they were treating me like an equal and
taking me to these neat places, introducing me to what I thought was absolutely
high society cool stuff. It was totally cool, are you kidding? I mean, little sister
finally gets acknowledged. I got to go too. It was fantastic. It was great. Did I
think Myra was terrific? *Yes.* I mean, they allowed me to come. Not all the
time, but they would invite me and I got all dressed up and went with them.

Oh, I had some other secrets too. I had this guy, Tony. Tony was like this
absolutely fantastic-looking Hispanic guy who had the most exquisitely chiseled,

beautiful face I could ever imagine. And he was absolutely off-limits from every point of view and I snuck off and saw him and was just wildly sexual with him, and *no one* knew. I sure didn't bring him home to my mother; no one in Vogue knew; he was a complete sexual secret. That was another piece of my life.

Tony was the main nonwhite person I came into contact with in any kind of meaningful way, and I hid him from everybody. It would have been absolutely not okay.

When I was a senior, I had really turned toward wanting to go to Stephens College, which was an all-girls college in Missouri. I wanted to go to Stephens for two reasons, and, again, they were secret passions. One was that they had a good equestrian program: horseback riding. The other was that they supposedly had a good literature program. Another deal was, for me, when I was a late junior and all through my senior year, again, spurred by this teacher, I moved from a forever C and D student--even in grammar school--to an A student. It's like I had *found* my intellect. So anyway, I didn't have the grades to get in until I was a senior. It's like I realized by that time that there was another world out there, and it was a world of ideas, a world of sophistication, and I was sort of a half-assed pretend beatnik. Jazz, and classical music--there was just a whole world out there that I didn't know about, that was much more attractive to me than this white gloves, pouring tea, getting married world. By the time I was a senior I envisioned myself as being a sort of poet or writer or intellectual, and I dressed in black, which was not cool, you know. That was what I had hoped for.

I remember, too, that by the time I turned away from Vogue my father died, and I'm sure that piece has a part in all this. My father died when I was sixteen, while I was a junior. There was some kind of freeingness about that. I could not get back into that frivolous stuff. I just got more serious altogether.

So, anyway, from my junior year until I got pregnant, I was filled with a sense of power and strength that I had never experienced. And I didn't exactly know where it was going to lead. But I knew what I didn't want. And I just had this glimmering, this taste that there was something out there that was more than the accepted girl thing to do. And Vogue didn't support that at all. The Dirty Seven did. Somehow, I could do that with the Dirty Seven and they would not turn from me.

Boys had a totally different initiation. One of the things we girls were taught-- one of the little ritual trips we learned--was how to start a conversation and carry it. In other words, how to ask the right kind of questions and say the right kind of stuff to appear very interested in what the guy was talking about. Whether you were or not! The deal was, saying, "Tell me more!" "That's very interesting!" In other words, drawing the guy out and making him feel important was part of what we learned how to do. That was part of the mating game. That was our job. As far as how you moved onward to marriage and the 'burbs: the women knew every step of the way. You knew that avocado green was in, and that you would have a shower, and what to ask for in the shower and how to set up your house, what to do when babies started crying--this was all handed down. People were already getting married in their senior year. We're talking seventeen, eighteen years old. The showers and marriages were already happening; the apartments. You knew to go to Akron to get all your shit to start out; it didn't seem unfamiliar. You didn't think about "relationships." Nobody talked about that. What the fuck was that? You just knew you were in love and it was gonna last forever and you had all these things to do. There were these little markers about how, then, to proceed from these marriages into successful, whatever, *adulthood*. There were these certain things that you did. And accumulated. It was about doing and having. Doing and having! Not feeling and thinking! Nobody talked about this stuff! No! You just didn't! You just believed that if you followed the right path, you were in love, that it was all gonna happen, that's all. You did what you were supposed to do and it was gonna happen. That was the disillusionment. Because it didn't happen. You did what you were supposed to do, and it didn't happen. So uh oh. Now what?

Vogue club photograph. Los Angeles High School, summer 1956.

Myra Schiller
W'56 President

Golda Tritschler
W'56 Vice President

Agnes Bryant
W'56 Secretary

George Takei
W'56 President

W'56 Senior Boards

Kneeling: Sandy Rogoff, Gilda Meyers Myra Schiller, Golda Tritschler, Agnes Bryant. **First Row:** Linda Kroweck, Marilyn Kieweg, Harriet Kearns, Edna Benford, Margaret Yukl, Marianne Levee, Jackie McLaughlin. **Second Row:** Sydney Kramer, Phyllis Nevins Pam Biggs, Barbara Lande, Rochelle Herson, Marilyn Wolley, Sandy Hershberg, Sandy Ruppert. **Third Row:** Liz Golden, Dani Budd, Amy Okamoto, Harriet Levy, Arline Lande, Pat Davenport. **Fourth Row:** Sharon Adler, Harriet Kramer, Nona Hodges, Carole Graves, Shirley Braginsky, Judy Kadushin, Sharon Brewster, Jackie Benton.

Kneeling: Mr. Reedy, Tommy Grossman, Cecil McLinn, Ron Schaffer, George Takei, Sal Osio. **First Row:** John Perlstein, Sanford Chapman, Marty Katz, Lee Young, Marty Rosenthal, Myron Bromberg. **Second Row:** Dave Soghor, George Wolfberg, Frank Meyer, Mike Bagnasarian, Ed Greenbaum, Burt Pines, Peter Rony, Jerry Nemetz. **Third Row:** Steve Saikin, Steve Lazar, Doug Tamkin, Dick Nathanson, Gary Dubin, Jack Bradshaw, Morty Berlin, Clark Neher. **Fourth Row:** Johnny Gutman, Paul Martin, Dennis Dailey, Joe Friedman, Jan Tempelaar-Lietz, Hans von Briesen, Rene Gelber, Bob Zide.

Myra Schiller and George Takei (Star Trek's Mr. Sulu), Senior Board Presidents of L.A. High School, 1956.

Baronettes club portrait.

Baronettes (Myra and Ellen) club portrait.

Baronettes (Myra and Ellen) club portrait.

Baronettes (Myra and Ellen) club portrait.

HISTORY OF THE DONATELLOS

It was in October of 1948 when six girls joined together to form the "Donatellos," a social and charitable organization. The club has now expanded to thirty members and twenty-one alumni.

Donatello is a famous Italian sculptor who excelled in his work during the Renaissance period. The name itself signifies "Lovers of Fine Art."

Many charitable affairs have been presented by the Donatellos. The "Sock Hop" in November of 1948, "Deep Purple" in June of 1949, and in February of 1950, one of the season's most successful dances, "Moonlight Magic."

In collaboration with the Cardinals we now present "Two in Tune." The entire proceeds from this venture will be given to the City of Hope, a cancer and tuberculosis foundation. We sincerely hope that this evening will long be remembered as one of happiness to you all. Thank you.

—DONATELLOS.

Officers

Adele Richman	*President*
Diane Skolnik	*Vice President*
Sheila Lerner	*Recording Secretary*
Mimi Gold	*Corresponding Secretary*
Corinne Miller	*Treasurer*
Mona Wenk	*Historian*
Elaine Lewin	*Sgt. at Arms*
Marlene Sinker	*Chaplain*

DONATELLOS

Darlene Albert	Phyllis Goldfine	Elaine Rubin
Joan Baum	Sheila Lerner	Beverly Schwartz
Lenore Brown	Elaine Lewin	Judy Shacter
Roberta Brown	Sara Mann	Marlene Sinker
Ethel Edelstein	Corinne Miller	Rocky Sitron
Sandy Familian	Sandy Rabin	Diane Skolnik
Sheila Fenton	Cecile Rayburn	Nina Solomon
Lenore Foss	Adele Richman	Mona Wenk
Joannie Golcon	Carol Rodin	Mimi Winston
Mimi Gold	Barbara Rubin	

One of the top Jewish girls' clubs at Fairfax High School.

In the summer of 1947, a group of eight determined girls organized a club, which they named "Tantras," meaning Greek Goddesses of Mystery. Our club has expanded until today we claim 24 active members and 38 alumni.

The main reasons for unification were to promote friendship, participate in social activities and most important of all, to contribute our time and efforts in the interests of charity. We are now an auxiliary of the City of Hope, a non-sectarian tubercular and cancer foundation.

Great progress and popularity have also been obtained from the success of the Tantras' four past financial ventures. They include "Lollipop Leap" in June of 1948, and our three huge semi-formal affairs: "Moonlight Minuet" in February, 1949, "Charity Dance" in February, 1950, and our extremely successful "Blue Heaven," which was presented last year.

Tonight, in conjunction with the Barons, we present to you our second "Blue Heaven" dance, which we hope will be another in a long line of successes.

✳

TANTRA OFFICERS W'52

President .CLAIRE FINLAY
Vice President. . . . . .JULIE BURNS
Recording Secretary . . . . .SALLY KAPLAR
Corresponding Secretary . . . . .BUNNY HARVITZ
Treasurer. . . . . .MYRNA GELDIN
Historian . . . . .EVELYN ZLOTKIN
Social Chairman. . . . . .LORRAINE BARRY
Sergeant-at-Arms. . . . . .JILL KENT

An early photo of the club Helen joined at Fairfax High School.

Exactly who the founding-fathers of the Barons were is lost in the dusty pages of history. We do know, however, that the later-to-be-famous name BARONS first echoed thru the hallowed halls and verdant campus of Fairfax Hi in the spring of the year 1936. Through the years many illustrious names have graced the numerous pages of our membership rolls.

The objectives of our organization are to promote social, fraternal, and philanthropic activities among the members. Some of the club's outstanding traditions are a strong feeling of brotherhood, sacredness of the Baron medallion and high standards of admission. Having been active in school leadership and athletics, the Barons have established a position of prominence.

Tonight, in conjunction with the Tantras, we are presenting our fifth charity dance.

✳

BARON OFFICERS W'52

President.....................ALEX AXELRODE
Vice President................FRED HALPRIN
Secretary......................NEIL KOWITT
Treasurer......................LEN RAPPING
Historian ....JOE ROTTMAN
Sergeant-at-Arms ....HERB ALPERT

Herb Alpert's club at Fairfax High School.

Fantasy in Gold

THE HISTORY OF THE CUBADONS

There were eleven girls who founded the Cubadons (meaning Little People) in July, 1946. The girls did so in order to work for other little people at the Children's Hospital. The original group of eleven has expanded into thirty-five active Cubadons and sixty alumnae. The Cubadons were organized mainly to enable the girls to work as a group in the interest of charity.

In 1948 our semi-formal dance "Portrait in Pink" was a huge success. Three years ago along with the Tantras, we presented our "Charity Dance" which will long be remembered as one of the finest dances given by two Fairfax clubs. Our most recent dance "Springtime" given in May, 1951, with all proceeds going to Mt. Sinai Cancer Clinic was also a huge success. We feel, also, that we have lived up to our reputation of being one of the most friendly and sincere clubs at Fairfax.

At this time we wish to thank all those who have worked to make this dance successful tonight. The proceeds of our "Fantasy in Gold" will go to the City of Hope. It is our fond hope that this dance proves to be one of the most outstanding affairs of the year.

Judy Ackerman	Joy Gold	Elaine Levoff
Barbara Atlas	Sandy Goldscher	Phyllis Marks
Corky Bloom	Iris Granz	Loretta Misraje
Carol Borman	Rosalie Greenberg	Cookie Morris
Harriet Cohen	Elaine Gross	Shelia Rubin
Carolyn De Sure	Gail Holleck	Sharon Rush
Sandy Fisher	Betty Hyman	Stara Sack
Cindy Fisher	Darlene Jaman	Natalie Salsburg
Jackie Fleisher	Marilyn Klein	Bobbie Sampson
Janice Friedman	Sandy Kohn	Sandy Silverman
Irene Garbus	Sharon Kosloff	Corky Walshin
Joan Clazer		Linda Wendell

CUBADONS

OFFICERS W'53

President	Nat Salsburg
Vice President	Barbara Atlas
Recording Secretary	Corrine Walshin
Corresponding Secretary	Carol Borman
Treasurer	Sandy Goldscher
Historian	Darlene Jaman
Chaplain	Carol De Sure
Sgt. at Arms	Betty Hyman
Pledge Mother	Iris Granz
Dance Chairman	Shelia Rubin
Dance Treasurer	Sharon Kosloff

A Jewish girls' club presents its history in a dance program at Fairfax High School.

THE HISTORY OF THE CARDINALS

In the spring of 1947, a small group of boys formed a club based on friendship and athletics. They called themselves the "Cardinals" and chose as their colors blue and white.

Upon entering high school, the "Cardinals" found that a socially-activated club succeeded more than merely an athletic club. Therefore as tenth graders they gave their first charity dance, "Midnight Rendez-vous." Last April in collaboration with the Vi Queens they presented "Flower Fantasy," their second charity dance.

As the club took in new members the boys began taking part in school activities, until now there are numerous lettermen from all sports and many student body officers in the "Cardinals."

Tonight with the Donatellos we present to you "Two in Tune." We hope that you will enjoy this evening as much as we have enjoyed putting forth our efforts to bring it to you.

Gary Jubas ....*President*
Les Cooper ....*Vice-President*
Buzz Engelson ....*Secretary*
Joe Siegal ....*Sgt. at Arms*
Len Jaffe ....*Pledge Mother*
Don Tronstein ....*Outgoing Treasurer*
Bob Pynes ....*Ingoing Treasurer*

CARDINALS

Mel Allan
*Larry Annenburg
Mort Bellet
*Mickey Borofsky
Bob Brownstein
*Lee Brownstein
Les Cooper
*Sherman Doctrow
Harvey Dorn
"Buzz" Engelson
Jack Epstein
*Dave Golden
*Norm Gosenfeld
Len Jaffe

Gary Jubas
*Wally Kaplar
Myron Kessler
Jack Kopel
Irv Laxineta
*Bill Machinoff
Roger Morris
Phil Neiman
Bob Pynes
*Bob Rutkin
*Phil Rabin
*Joe Ruby
Bob Roischan
*Murray Schwimmer

Sherwin Shayne
Fred Seigal
Joe Seigal
*Aaron Silvera
Marco Silvera
Al Silvers
Sandy Simons
*Jerry Spitz
Don Tronstein
Jerry Tronstein
*Bob Zacky
*Rick Janis

*Alumni

Roger's club history—From a dance program.

CUBADONS

Best Wishes

for a Successful Dance

the

TANTRAS

Officers W'52-53

President .... Carol Turitz
Vive President .... Lorraine Barry
Recording Secretary .... Marsha Edelstek
Corresponding Secretary .... Sandy Krull
Treasurer .... Rochelle Barenfeld
Historian .... Carol Walbert
Social Chairman .... Terry Malin
Sgt. at Arms .... Sandy Fredlander
Chaplain .... Veronica Carey

Good Luck Cubadons

on Your Fantasy In Gold

THE

BARONS

Officers W'52-53

President .... Joel Rottman
Vice President .... Fred Halprin
Secretary .... Fred Santo
Treasurer .... Herb Alpert
Sgt. at Arms .... Jerry Hodes

Top Jewish clubs, male and female, at Fairfax High School. Note that musician Herb Alpert, who went on to found A&M Records, began as the Baron's treasurer.

Jewish clubs at Fairfax High School congratulate each other.

OUR SINCEREST CONGRATULATIONS
ON THE SUCCESS OF YOUR DANCE

COLONIAL SUB DEBS

Congratulations and Best Wishes
On Your Dance

Sires

Pres.	George Levine
V. Pres.	Al Bass
Sec.	Art Schonfeld
Treas.	Jerry Kovacs

BEST WISHES ON YOUR WONDERFUL DANCE

The Templars

STAGS HI-Y

Les Kaufman	Pres.
Rudy Michaelis	V. Pres.
Al Thomson	Treas.
Hutch Beckner	Sec.
George Niota	Sgt. at Arms

Bernie Beckner	Marty Goldstein
Stan Finkenstein	Gerry Holzman
Joe Rivara	Don Lippman
Russ Barnes	Phil Presber
Saul Bernstein	Al Silberman
Dave Aldemar	Don Wedermann
Murrie Chessmore	Al Weinroth

Sample club ads from Fairfax High School clubs—all Jewish.

WESTERN UNION

1201

W. P. MARSHALL, PRESIDENT.

SYMBOLS

DL = Day Letter
NL = Night Letter
LC = Deferred Cable
NLT = Cable Night
Ship Radiogram

The filing time shown in the date line on telegrams and day letters is STANDARD TIME at point of origin. Time of receipt is STANDARD TIME at point of destination

KEEEK XX LLC011-601 NL PD
LOS ANGELES CAL. 30

MYRA SHILLER
APPT. E-2 766 AUGUSTA, ST.
WEST COLUMBIA, S. C.

DEAR MYRA WE CORDIALY INVITE YOU TO PLEDGE BARONETTES GROUP

REPLY BEFORE EIGHT AM BY MAIL NOV. 2ND. TO 1307½ SOUTH HIGHLAND

LOVE.

BARONETTES.

Sample telegraph mailed to Myra, inviting her to pledge the Baronettes club.

We the

Barons   and   Tantras

HERB ALPERT	ROCHELLE BARENFIELD	FANYA GREENWALD
ALEX AXELRODE	LORRAINE BARRY	BUNNY HARVITZ
FARREL BROSLAWSKY	JUDY BERMAN	SALLY KAPLAR
FRED HALPERIN	JULIE BURNS	JILL KENT
NEIL KOWITT	RANDY CEASON	SANDY MARKS
SAM LEEPER	JACKIE COHEN	LYN MYERS
FRED LERNER	BARBARA CUTLER	NANCY MOSS
JERRY MELLS	BARBARA EDELBERG	INEX NEWMAN
RALPH MICHAEL	MARSHA EDELSACK	DIANE PANNISH
MURRAY OZER	CLAIRE FINLEY	CAROL TURITZ
AL PAPPE	IRENE GARBUS	ARLENE WAXMAN
LENORD RAPPING	MYRNA GELDIN	EVELYN ZLOTKIN
JOE ROTTMAN	ELLEN GOODMAN	
MERV RUSH		

...sincerely thank you for your attendance. We hope that, through our efforts, you have had an enjoyable evening.

La Cienega and Melrose Flower Shop

CLUB CORSAGES A SPECIALTY

JOE COHN, MANAGER

Best Wishes on a Successful Dance

"The Cardinals"

President..............DON TRONSTEIN
Vice President................PHIL BELOUS
Corresponding Secretary.....IRV LAXANETTA
Recording Secretary..............MEL ALLAN
Treasurer.......................JACK KOPOL
Sergeant-at-Arms ....STAN BELCHIK

A Barons/Tantras dance program.

BEST WISHES FOR A SUCCESSFUL DANCE

CERELEDS OF L. A. 'HI

Pres.	Syd Meltzer
V. Pres.	Marian Kahn
Sec.	Teddy Loplitsky
Treas.	Sylvia Kahane
Advisor	JoAnn Segal
Sponsor	Mrs. Roseman

PARAGONS

Pres.	Ron Bloom
V. Pres.	Walt Zaslove
Sec.	Bob Schwartz
Treas.	Ben LaBarsky

Mel Appel   Bob Gerst
Dave Braveman   Dick Guttman
Phill Dunn   Mal Fienberg
Arnie Familian   Stan Hyman

Nov. 12   Nov. 12

At every party remember this treat
Tom Sawyer Potato Chips can't be beat
They're crisp, fresh, the best in the West.
You'll agree if you give them a test.

SERVE TOM-SAWYER POTATO CHIPS

EDGEMAR FARMS

CHOICE DAIRY PRODUCTS

SINCE 1880

Telephones:

EXbrook 6-3165   TExas 0-3771
ARizona 9-7705   STate 0-4241

Club dance program, L.A. High School.

Fantasy in Gold

Best Wishes from

TAU DELTA PHI

U.C.L.A.

Watch for

"THE CHASE"

in May

Bigger and Better Than Ever

CUBADONS

Best wishes are in hand,
To a group that's really grand.

We know your dance will be great.
As a club the Cubadons really do rate.

So good luck, best wishes are really in hand.
Your annual club dance will turn out grand!

THE DONATE'LLOS . . . .

President .... Sara Mann
Vice President .... Barbara Roslaw
Recording Secretary .... Elaine Rubin
Corresponding Secretary .... Lila Winston
Treasurer .... Toni Kestenburg
Chaplain .... Judy Schacter

And Members

Sample club dance program. Note the U.C.L.A. fraternity ad, recruiting L.A. High School students.

CUBADONS

CARDINALS

PRESENT

AZURTE'

FEATURING

**Mel Erwin
and His Orchestra**

𝔉𝔞𝔫𝔱𝔞𝔰𝔶 𝔦𝔫 𝔊𝔬𝔩𝔡

BARONETTES

RACQUET - CLUB

January 24

Guest Stars

Entertainment

Sample dance program: Cardinals and Baronettes club dance events.

We knew your dance would be just great
To be here we could hardly wait
Of "TWO IN TUNE" we'll dream in sleep
Hope to see you at the "LEVI LEAP."

Congratulations

THE ZEPHS

"REMEMBER MARCH 17"

MAY YOUR DANCE
BE A GREAT SUCCESS

DOMINOES

BEST OF LUCK AND SUCCESS ON YOUR DANCE

THE DEVRONS

Pres. ....Terry Stark
V. Pres. ....Elaine Alberkrack
Sec. ....Charnette Firestein
Treas. ....Arlene Margolis
Historian ....Judy Penn
Sgt. of Arms ....Lita Margolis

THE CHALDEANS

Extend Heartiest Congratulations to the
CARDINALS AND DONATELLOS
on their "Two In Tune,"

which we know will be a tremendous success

Pres. ....Audrey Weiss
V. Pres. ....Iris Miller
Corr. Sec. ....Leah Lizer
Res. Sec. ....Helene Stein
Treas. ....Carol Golding
Hist. ....Carol Zavat
Sgt. at Arms ....Gerry Fein
Chaiplan ....Ruby Greenberg

Dance programs featuring ads from Fairfax High School clubs.

Best Wishes and
Congratulations to the
CARDINALS AND DONATELLOS
ON YOUR DANCE

DELTA PI

Pres. .... Shirley Gummelson
Vice Pres. .... Sylvia Werslow
Sec. .... Susan Hilbert
Treas. .... Sharon Clardy
Lust. .... Shirley Anderson
Soc. Chr. .... Judy Guffey

Best Wishes
on "TWO IN TUNE"

Orions
OF L. A. HI

THE

Cardinals & Donatellos

PROUDLY PRESENT

"Two in Tune"

AT THE

Riviera Country Club

FEBRUARY 21, 1951

PROCEEDS TO THE CITY OF HOPE

A Fairfax High School club dance. Held at a country club in 1951. Note ad from a club at L.A. High School in the dance program.

4

Jennifer

As a toddler, Jennifer escaped from Nazi Europe with her Jewish parents, one of whom had already been imprisoned in a concentration camp. Her experiences as a teenager at L.A. High were framed in this tension of immigrant refugee status. Longing to fit in, Jennifer joined Myra's club: the Baronettes. Here, she hoped she would learn how to be "more American," and, most importantly, "have a place to stand in the schoolyard" when the different clubs staked out their social turf at lunchtime and recess.

Although she longed for the Baronettes' glamour to rub off on her, Jennifer was also critical of the club's "cheap" behavior and resented the Baronettes' ease with boys [Myra's confidence and popularity in particular]. The club offered little to satisfy Jennifer's identity as an intellectual, emphasizing instead the importance of appearing attractive to men. Yet it was Jennifer who succeeded in marriage while remaining true to her interests, finding, early on, a loving husband who has also been her intellectual companion. And despite their adolescent rivalry, Myra and Jennifer remained friends for decades after leaving L.A. High, sharing family outings throughout their child-rearing years.

This interview took place in Jennifer's car on the Hollywood Freeway as we drove back from visiting her son at his movie studio office. Where Jennifer struggled to fit into the American image in the 1950s, her children are now American image makers in the 1990s.

I was born in Hungary. My family was named after an old city in Hungary; Jews were often given the names of cities, to identify them. I came here when I was a year and a half old. My father was held in one of the most notorious concentration camps, and we got out on the *last boat out of Holland*. My father came here and he couldn't speak English, and he used to walk to work wearing a suit, and pretend that he had taken the streetcar. He didn't have a dime for the streetcar.   So we were really very poor.   But my father always wanted to *do* everything to help me fit in, and I always got the best.

My mother worked at a big department store; she worked at Clifton's on the line at the cafeteria. Both my parents were truly poor immigrants. My father had an eighth-grade education, yet he would talk about Shakespeare. And my father always said that he began reading Shakespeare when he was nine years old. So, when I was in high school and going out with a guy in college, and I told him that I was reading Dostoevsky, my father yelled from the house "Ahh, I read that when I was ten!" My father was very intellectual.

My mother tried hard to become an American. For my thirteenth birthday I had a party at my house. My American aunts and uncles came over and told my mother to serve the grapefruit with the toothpicks, and the olives at the end. That was a very big thing, grapefruits with toothpicks stuck in them. Very American, like store-bought mayonnaise. They made all this and I got my period and went to sleep. I went upstairs and they had the party without me. It was humiliating. It was horrible; I had such cramps I could not stand up. And my mother--I wanted her to do things the American way, and she didn't know how. And there are some people who can do those things naturally? And it's funny. People meet my mother now, and they think she's so smart, so political.

So, my parents were from Hungary. My mother was somebody who didn't fit in here, and, *I* felt, didn't know how to do things right; always was terribly uncomfortable. And I felt that, until really recently--I don't feel this way anymore--but for nearly thirty years, I was looking for role models. I read women writers, and then those Baronettes were my role models. Except they were so *dumb!* So *boring!* And that was the problem.

First I went to John Burroughs [junior high school]. It's funny because I don't even remember Myra then. I wasn't friends with her in junior high school. I met her in high school, that's right, and I don't even remember how I did meet her in high school. My club in junior high school was called the Burrows, and I don't remember what happened with that club.

I always thought of myself as smart. That was very, very important to me. But I also wanted to be beautiful. And I think I had a pretty good body, but I wasn't beautiful; I *knew* I wasn't beautiful. My mother was beautiful; I didn't look like my mother, I looked like my father. Okay. I thought of myself as smart. As for the three clubs at L.A. High, the Sans Souci were like average nice girls, and I wanted to join a club probably because I cared about being in the mainstream, and being popular, and that's what people in clubs were.

It never occurred to *me* to join a Gentile club, or to act Gentile, like Myra did. She, I felt, would have fit in with those people. I felt like there were some people who crossed over--like Sue. It was almost like whites, like a white and a black line, and I felt Myra was one of the people who could have crossed over. She was very involved with school activities; that made her a little bit purer, you know, all that. And even though she was involved with service, she also was someone who gave a lot as far as activities, and she was also a "good girl"...*which I never trusted!* Ha ha! I never quite trusted that good girl part. But she always appeared that way, and that was her persona. And I felt that way about her; I felt that she could *pass*. And I never thought of myself that way.

I thought I would go into one of these three [Jewish] clubs. I didn't get into Dantes. I remember thinking I probably wouldn't get in, and the reason, I felt-- this is what I felt and is probably just an excuse--was that my family wasn't wealthy and I also wasn't involved in school activities. So I didn't have that extra, other dimension that I felt you needed. And I was, ah, I don't think I ever fit in anyplace. But the Baronettes, I thought, well, I liked the idea of being with the beautiful people. The Sans Souci seemed boring. But I felt like maybe this magic of being beautiful, because there is a magic about being that beautiful, would rub off on me in some way. What happened, which I think is so funny, is there was this one group of very beautiful women who were maybe two or three years ahead of me and when they graduated everybody became pretty plain-looking! Did Myra ever say anything about that?

Joining the Baronettes--when I went to college, I joined a sorority, which I quit after a year. And I had to go through horrible hazing and that's *vivid* to me. But I don't remember a thing from high school. We didn't have hazing; we had "scrolls." Oh my God, *I remember my big sister! What was her name?* I fixed Larry up with her! My husband, Larry, and I met each other when I was in my second year of college, and I fixed him up with her, and she was nice but *dumb*. So different from Larry. I mean, she--I shouldn't say this. I'm sounding so pejorative about these people--well, I fixed them up but, thank God, it didn't work out.

So I joined Baronettes and my big sister made me a scroll, and I didn't like *it or her*. These dumb scrolls--oy, I mean all this stuff is so *foreign*. And it was mawkishly sentimental, everything. And I don't know whether I thought it was sentimental or whether I thought it was *stupid*. I can't believe that I really liked any of that club stuff.

All I can remember were parties. You have to remember I wouldn't have done any of this stuff: flower arrangements, decorations, sandwich making, pouring tea. See, I would have thought all of it was such *bullshit*. I hated it. It was torture. I had very little to do with it. The whole thing was so alien to me. I was a sixties person--never a fifties person--except I loved the clothes. The whole thing with clothes: when you talk about surface, that was so important to me! And I've spent my *life* trying to negate that and get away from it!

I saved up my money to buy clothes at Jack Hansen's, very simple fifties style. I got a lot of clothes free because my uncle owned a company in the valley. His clothes were expensive but weren't what other kids wore; I didn't like them. I always felt as if I didn't fit in because I would wear a lot of those clothes. He sold to Nieman Marcus. I wanted to buy what everyone else had. In junior high school, I owned three sweaters and like three skirts. And every night my best friend would figure out what I should wear so I could mix them up and make them look new every day, maybe a new scarf. We always wore scarves. They don't wear those teensy little scarves today. Oh, God--oh, oh, oh--I had these *great* see-through plastic shoes! Three-inch heels. They were Lucite in the back and Lucite in the front. And then I had a purse, a Lucite purse. Back then, it all meant so little to me that eventually I gave my purse away as tacky. Now it would be a collector's item.

We wore long earrings, and there was that look of *whimsy,* but I don't think we thought of it as whimsy. We took it very seriously. People, now, are looking really to make fun of everything in the fifties; none of this was funny at the time. You had your plastic purse, your Lucite bag, you put your scarf in it--I guess we looked about twenty-six years old. I know that I used an eyelash curler and I used mascara and I used rouge. When you see a picture of me I look absolutely characterless. There is nothing about me that can tell you something about who that person is, in all the pictures, almost. And it's just astonishing to me.

I think of school, in general, as having been very painful. And I was in conformity-land, and I conformed, but I wasn't happy. I wanted to learn how to be an American, and those were the role models that I chose.

I was often angry at Myra. She got away with wearing forbidden things because she seemed like such a nice person. She was this goody-goody person, and she used to wear half-slips when you were supposed to wear full slips. That was a law, that was a school rule, that you had to wear a full slip, *God forbid* you should show! You had to cover your whole body, and Myra would wear a half-slip and she got away with it. And *she* was the girls' Senior Board vice president, who gave out citations for breaking school dress code rules! And I always felt that she was able to seem like a good girl *and* avoid bullshit rules too. How it pissed me off! I didn't get dress citations; but I got in trouble for talking too much. I used to get A, U, U on my report card: unsatisfactories in conduct.

The full slip was such a big deal. You weren't allowed to see anything; you couldn't see your bra. That was a big rule. You weren't allowed to smoke, and I did smoke. I started smoking at fifteen in the Baronettes. Everybody smoked. I have the feeling that this rule was written down, but I don't know where.

I thought the Baronettes were very fast. They were considered very fast. Myra didn't really fit into this group at all. I don't think I fit in. In fact, I think this whole pledge class were really a bunch of freaks. We were just misfits. I was a misfit because I thought that the life of the mind was more important than anything else. Except that I had a problem with *looks;* I was hung up on looks. But Myra, because she was so involved with school activities, she didn't fit in: these people didn't do anything like that. Myra was really a doer, and she did get things done.

And also I thought of these people as on the edge of being "cheap girls," quote, right? I mean, I didn't think of them as being whores, but they were cheap. If they went out, what would they let a guy do? Feel them up? What would they do? I have no idea what I thought they would do. I don't know if I thought they would sleep with somebody or not. They might. In high school

I thought that sex was fun, and I enjoyed it. I didn't like a lot of the restrictions. But I didn't sleep with anybody.

I remember that I fixed up this college guy--because I went out with all these college guys--with a girl who was in one of the less popular clubs. *I* fixed her up, and she got pregnant. That was a real *schanda*. And she left school. This was a terrible thing. You know, now, somebody might be pregnant and finish school; she left school. I don't know whether she married him, or what happened. That was really something, a big deal.

A lot of college guys went out with high school girls. And I would have liked to go out with high school guys, too, but I felt so much *older* than they were. And that's what's so interesting about Myra: is that she was able to go out with these guys. She looked much older; she would dance with people up to her chin, be totally comfortable with it and very, very nice. Comfortable with herself, too, so that she could do that. She felt good enough about herself even if she was with a nerdy guy. I felt so uncomfortable with these guys coming up and flirting with me. I didn't know how to respond, because I knew it wasn't for real; it was bullshit. I was uncomfortable--and envious. Because I would have liked to go out with these guys in high school. And Myra met them through her school activities. And I wasn't involved in that. I always worked.

I worked in the summer, and when I went to college I worked while I went to school. And the sorority was just a catastrophe for me. It was just awful. I don't think I do well in groups. First of all, I think it's hard for me to be a part of the group and not stand out. I was an only child; I always wanted attention; I remember going to Hollywoodland Camp in junior high school and I clicked my teeth with my fingernails at night, so nobody could go to sleep, and I would lie in bed and laugh my head off and they couldn't *stand* me! And it's funny because I don't remember them feeling that way about me in high school. I didn't make people unable to stand me in high school. In college, I remember, again making jokes at the wrong time. But it was very serious in high school and I was scared of those older kids. And there were a lot of rules aside from the whole slip! That one was the most egregious. But also you weren't allowed to wear dividers. And there were people who got away with them.

I had a crush on a Mexican guy who was so gorgeous. And I remember that that was forbidden. Or that was for people like Sue, but not me. I couldn't and I *wouldn't* have crossed the line to that Mexican guy; I was too conventional. And too frightened, even though he was the sexiest guy I had ever seen. I could see girls doing that in the other clubs; they were not Jews! I'm sure there was more class mobility there.

I think that it had to do with the men too: that the Jewish guys, if they found out you were fast, they wouldn't marry you or be interested in you. I was sure, if I slept with somebody, that no one would ever marry me. Oh, yeah. I also would have a very hard time lying about something like that, where a lot of people wouldn't. I mean, nobody tells everything. We all know that.

How were the Baronettes prepared to become wives? Well, the reason *I* was going to college was so I could be smart enough to fuck--and to *marry*--the kind of man who I wanted. That was the reason. I was very interested in ideas, but part of that was that I wanted to discuss them with my future mate. And being smart was very important to me. And I learned later that it was *overly* important to me. Because I didn't think I really *was* smart, because my father told me how stupid women were. And he put my mother down every minute he could. He probably thought I should go to school to marry the kind of man I wanted; he didn't think of work as success.

And so when I went to college, I majored in apparel merchandising because I wanted to be a buyer. I was so interested in clothes, that was a natural. And in high school I worked at Bullocks; I was head of the Davy Crockett thing. I wore a hat and sang, "Davy, Davy Crockett, King of the Wild Frontier." I was very good at selling; I used to play the ukelele. I ran the department, when the fad was falling apart, when people didn't want those damn hats anymore. Anyway, I thought, I'll be a buyer in a department store, and then I'll go to college as a merchandising major. I had to take sewing, which I was a failure at; I hated it. And I was in the art department, and I didn't know anything about art, but that was a wonderful accident. And then I had to take accounting. I still have nightmares, and did for years, about flunking accounting. Finally I said I don't care that my father wants to prepare me for something, I'm going to become an English major. So I became an English major, and then I was *so happy. So happy!* But it didn't prepare me to *do* anything! I never thought I would *have* to do anything! It never occurred to me! I was preparing myself to be able to attract somebody; I was reading all these books, and that really was numero uno.

It was more than being sufficiently educated. I wanted somebody very special. *And I got him.* I really did. I got such a brilliant and interesting man, who delights me every day. I mean, nothing is perfect, and marriage is a lot of work, but I was really lucky. But most people who had that dream, it didn't work for. So.

About the Baronettes: I was so unhappy in that club. But where would I have gone if I had dropped out? I would have been a nothing. I would have been one of those people who didn't have any place to stand, you know. The clubs had certain places that they stood at breaks in school. And you know, it was so nice to be among this very beautiful group of women. To be like them, and, Sans Souci had their group and Dantes were over there, I even remember where they were. They would all be together. Did Myra talk about that? And then the Anoras, that club, that terrible club. They were treated like the dogs of the Jewish clubs.

I was vice president of the senior class. I finally ran for something. See, most of the time I was unable to run because I got "unsatisfactories" in behavior. I was always in trouble for talking. Always. I was always trying to get attention and it was a terrible problem; I didn't know how I would do in college, but they had such big classes in college that I was better off. So, finally I shut my mouth enough so that I had a semester where I didn't get a U. I couldn't run for a student body office because I had the U's. So I ran, and it was so sad; I got this terrible case of acne. I'm sure that having to do all this work was very stressful for me. I had to do the Senior Prom. And the woman who I'd lost to? I made her my prom chairman. She did a lot of the work; in fact, most of the work. And at the end, an award is given to the person who is the vice president? I didn't get it. *They gave it to her.* And I remember a friend of mine feeling just terrible and standing up for me. She had a kind of integrity; she felt this was a wrong thing to do and she stood up for me, and I was so impressed with that. To have that kind of integrity, and go against people, and stand up for people. It wasn't that she was such a good friend of mine either. She was a friend. But it was that she felt this was wrong, and it was wrong. It was very hurtful.

And the prom was fabulous and I went with this guy I was going with who was at UCLA. I still have my dress. You want to see it? I wore lavendar, with little spaghetti straps, and it was made of chiffon, I had it made. With this huge skirt that was permanently pressed pleats. And of course you wore a Merry Widow; everyone wore Merry Widows. I don't know if *Myra* wore one. A Merry Widow was a big fifties thing! It's a bra with stays that goes all the way down to your waist. And everybody wore it, to push up your boobs and make your waist look smaller. And then you wore slips underneath it to make your skirts stand out. I still have it. That's something I kept. See, the clothes I kept. Funny. I didn't keep the shoes.

I don't think my mother understood. I mean, I did everything myself. How did I get to the place to go shopping? Did I take a bus? I didn't get my own car until I was in college. There were a lot of kids who had cars; I was very friendly with some kids who went to Fairfax. In fact, my best friends went to Fairfax and were Tantras. My best friend: she was such a wonderful person and she disappeared. And I think it had to do with our having less in common later on. Her parents were so nice; they were European Jews. I never got to know Myra's mother at all; she was also nice but I was scared of her. I don't know what it was. She had these beautiful daughters, and I didn't know her at all.

The whole thing with the Baronettes is like a hole; I don't remember. On weekends you went out. And you know there were rules when you went out. Like Larry asked me out, three weekends in a row. But you have to ask somebody out a week ahead of time. Because if you don't it means you're not popular, if you accept? So even though I wasn't busy I said I was busy. I wanted to seem popular. And even if I wasn't, he had some nerve to call me up and ask me out on a Friday for a Saturday night date. He didn't know the rules. He wouldn't have, because those things were very unimportant to him. Somebody from my culture would have known; he wasn't from my culture. He would have thought all that stuff was so stupid; that's why I fell in love with him.

He didn't know that on a first date you didn't take a girl to the beach. But he took me to the beach! You didn't do that except with a cheap girl! Girls like me didn't go to the beach to make out; we just didn't do that. I had these rigid rules. But I went with him on that first date to the beach. He gave me a kiss, and that was it. That was it! The best kiss. But that was when I was like nineteen years old. Also, he was short--I couldn't wear my Lucite three-inch heels. What was I going to do? I had to go and buy some new shoes for him, had to get special little two-inch heels, but that didn't look very sexy. So I went and I got myself Papagallos; that's when I started wearing Papagallos. *Now* I wear three-inch heels; I don't care if I'm taller. But there were those rules: you *only* went out with a guy that was taller than you; it was all so sad and rigid, and thank goodness it isn't like that anymore.

Myra, I think, bent some of those rules more than I did. I really think she did. What made me so mad was that she was able to do that and still look like a nice girl! It wasn't fair! She behaved like a saint but I *knew* she was a swinger, and it made me angry. Then she turned out to be this totally different, loving kind of person! But she was after every guy then. That's the way it was! I mean, this woman was *so involved* with guys and it was very important to her. It was important to all of us, but you know something? I think Myra did really like guys, and I think that they got that message. I don't think I liked them as much as she did. I think I was always more frightened. And I wanted smart guys.

I told Larry afterwards that he just didn't know, because he asked me out for the *same day*: asked me out on a Friday for a Saturday and I had to say I was busy for three weeks. He thought it was bullshit. Larry didn't know the rules. So he'd call Friday afternoon. And I'd say I was busy. "Look, maybe next week." So he'd call next Friday afternoon. The thing is that Larry didn't even know to be impressed that I was busy. Larry, did you know you were supposed to be impressed that I was busy? Did that turn you on, that you had this popular girl? It didn't. See, he didn't even know.

In high school I remember going cruising on Sunset Boulevard. I went in a car with some girls. I was so scared! Nobody was in the service then -- or were they? Was that the Korean War? There was a canteen on Sunset Boulevard, to entertain the troops. Maybe these girls were going to pick up guys? I was so scared that I actually sat on the floor of the car. Humiliating, too. I think I was with girls who were maybe cheap girls. There were the cheap girls, see, and the others. But it's so interesting. I'll bet you hear that more from me than you do from anybody else. They were girls who wanted boys. I could have, I was fascinated by it, but I was so scared! I think I was probably scared because I thought I would let myself go and something terrible would happen; I would go to hell or something; I would lose control.

We went to Tiny Naylor's, up on Sunset; that was great. I don't think there are any Tiny Naylor's left. There were a few of them and oh, I loved going there and looking at the people. Just sitting in the window--oh, I thought it was so exciting. And Delores Drive-In was a big hangout but I wasn't a part of these people. The guys I went out with were all in college so we went out on Friday and Saturday night. I was the one who was always fixing everybody up. And I was as obsessed with boys as Myra was. It's just that she was very, very successful.

If Myra set her sights on something, ay-yi-yi. What you would have to do was deflect the Evil Eye. But when Larry and I were going together she was gone. She was with Roger. *Thank God* Roger took her out of the competition! I think people competed a lot with Myra. She was totally the vamp, you know. I sound pretty nasty, but it's because I just wasn't tough. I remember Myra marrying a Gentile, and I was very happy that she had found somebody. At least she wasn't a threat any more! She was always nice, very nice, and always tried not to hurt anyone's feelings. But she just couldn't help it when boys came along. She *lost her mind!* She was like a *magnet!*

When I got ready to go on a date--oh, God! *Hours.* I remember that in high school I worked at Saks Fifth Avenue, taking care of the books and the beauty salon. And George Masters worked there. He was the guy who does all the movie people. So I would have my nails done; I mean, when I met Larry, I was as perfect as anybody could be. I was the kind of person who would *never* walk out with my hair in rollers. And I was so meticulous about myself.

I remember always being nervous and having to go to the bathroom. I remember every night going to bed with very very large curlers. And I slept on them. Huge curlers. Every night. And when I got married Larry told me I couldn't wear them anymore. Remember? And I had to figure out another way. He thought they were so horrible, so hideous. We didn't use curling irons; we used great big rollers.

What else did I do to get ready? I just know that it took a long time and it was very important. I only took baths. There was something wonderful about taking a bath. My mother washed my hair, for years. Jewelry was important. I had a silver necklace that was from Mexico, and some little bracelets that I wore a lot.

The Baronettes were cheap girls, and so I think maybe I looked down on Myra marrying a Gentile, a little bit, at first, because I didn't know how smart Roger was. He was very gorgeous. He was a *hunk!* He was, like, *amazing.* All I did was hear about it; I didn't know him. See, you have to remember that my father wouldn't let me go out with anybody that was Gentile. Absolutely not.

In high school, there was this lovely black guy, a jazz player, who had a new car and wanted to take me for a ride. My father wouldn't let me go. When my parents went away, I went to the beach--I was a beach rat--and there was a guy that I met who was a lifeguard. And I went out with him, while my parents were gone. He came to my house and was so excited to be going out with a Jewish girl--he knew they were great. So I went out with him and then cut it off; I wasn't that interested. But I think Gentiles were really *verboten.* I never thought of them. It was an area of men that just was not in my consciousness. I thought they were cute. But I didn't think they were smart enough.

When I think about the Gentile, I think of something that was forbidden. And something that was dangerous and scary. I was not secure enough, as an immigrant child, to fool around with that. That would besmirch me too much. The lifeguard, that was in high school. I don't remember his name. But I remember that I kissed him and I necked with him. He was very cute; I mean, he was a *lifeguard*. Of course I was sneaking out. But I was scared to death. What if my parents came home?

5

Helen and Bob

Helen and Myra did not attend the same high school; they met in their senior year through their boyfriends, who had been best friends since childhood. The two women then forged a friendship that has lasted to this day, including a ritual New Year's Eve phone call every year.

In contrast to Myra and Ellen's club ambivalence and self-conscious awareness of immigrant heritage, Helen hailed from a more settled and prosperous Jewish family and approached club life at Fairfax High School with pleasure and self-confidence. Helen was neither discontented nor rebellious during her adolescent years. Her role in the Tantras, a top Jewish girls' club, enabled her to observe and influence the school pecking order.

Helen is now married to Bob, also an alumnus of Fairfax High School.

Bob was often unhappy during his years at Fairfax High School. He brought both intellectual acuity and global living experiences to hallways where superficial qualities alone often determined popularity and club bids. In the beach culture of Southern California, Bob found himself excluded from the club scene and functioned as a Jewish "independent" at Fairfax. His sharp memories are a contrast to the easy glamour Roger enjoyed as a teenager at the same school.

However, the successful marriage of Bob and Helen brought together two Fairfax graduates who once occupied opposite ends of the social spectrum. Reconstructing their earlier selves, in the context of a present, loving relationship, allowed Bob and Helen to challenge one another's high school memories. Amused nostalgia and mock insults flew during this interview in their Los Angeles home. A central point of the conversation concerned, once again, the very different perspectives of male and female students in the 1950s. Bob was as familiar as Roger with the masculine sphere of beach crap games, sexual slang and exploits, oft-censored recordings by local black jazz musicians, and other "streetwise" phenomena completely unknown to Helen and Myra. The sheltering of "good girls" from the larger world available to their boyfriends is part of this past era's legacy of separate spheres and double standards for sexual initiation.

BOB: During the years '51-'54, everybody who was in the social swim was in a club. There were very few independents. There was a hierarchy. There were the clubs that had the more attractive and affluent, popular kids, and the ones who were less so. But there were a lot of kids who were not in any club--the nerds, the intellectuals, the uglies, the fatties, the me's. I was never asked to rush a club, I never got blackballed by a club, I had no relationship with a club. But most of my friends were in clubs, including some of the *preferred* boys' clubs. No one ever asked me if I wanted to join one, though. The Cardinals was a preferred club, and Roger was in that; the Barons; the Paragons; those are the only three I remember.

HELEN: If you weren't a Cardinal or a Baron or a Paragon it didn't matter what you were. You didn't matter.

BOB: All my friends in clubs were in those clubs. I was an only child and a bookworm and a very solitary kid. I had traveled all over the world, but I wasn't used to affiliating with a group scene of any kind and I never have been. I did join a fraternity in college, reluctantly. And I didn't identify with the fraternity at college. I wasn't really the club type, ever, so I wasn't a club *candidate.* Even if I'd been asked, which I wasn't.
   There was a pecking order. The kids in the clubs ate together. They had meetings. They had their own little cliques. The girls tended to prefer boys who were in clubs because that was a social badge. The clubs had their own dances off-campus. The thing that I recall about the clubs is exactly what I also recall about life in the '50s in fraternities at UCLA, which was very similar, and that is that you really cannot stereotype the kids in the clubs. There were kids in the clubs who were very ambitious, and who did their work in school, and took it very seriously, and knew when they were fifteen years old that they wanted to be a doctor or a dentist or a lawyer. Studying. And they could also be athletes, partying and chasing girls. It was very heterogeneous in the clubs. But I did not relate to the school. I was alienated from the school. And I didn't much approve of the club scene.
   So some of my friends were in clubs and some weren't. And I don't think the *guys* cared who was or was not in a club. And they may or may not have liked the other guys in the club. It was like any small group, thirty or forty people. So if you're looking at my class of six hundred boys and girls I would imagine that fewer than half were in a club; maybe a third or less. So it was no big deal not to be in a club. There were people who were intelligent, attractive, athletes, achievers who were not in clubs.

HELEN: Who were not in clubs?

BOB: Okay, Henry Aaron. You know who he is? University of Maryland, one of the top economists in the country in public policy. He was a friend of mine.

Most brilliant guy in the class at my high school? Henry was not in a club.

HELEN: That's right. Because if you were identified by intellect, if that was what identified you, that did not make you primary "club material." You'd have to be identified by your popularity, by your athletics, or by your looks. That's the way it was. Tell the truth.

BOB: But the primary recruitment for the clubs was just like recruitment for fraternities and sororities: it's the incoming class from junior high. In this case tenth grade.

HELEN: Right. And you know how they chose people?

BOB: By who was hot in the ninth grade.

HELEN: That's right. They had pictures, in our club, pictures of girls coming in from ninth grade.

BOB: So your ninth grade status determined your tenth grade recruitment by a club.

HELEN: It depends. You had a hierarchy of clubs. At Fairfax, you had the girls' clubs: I remember the Donatellos and the Tantras. And the Donatellos and the Tantras were divided. That's where people thought all the pretty girls were. There were some not so cute, but they were sisters of somebody.

BOB: That's called a legacy. They feel the responsibility to let you in the door.

HELEN: You know, you could get a relative in, too. So there were those two clubs, the Donatellos and the Tantras. Then there was the Zephs, and a variety of others. And the Zephs were very nice. But they weren't quite--they would be the B in looks.

BOB: I liked the Zephs. They were the girls that had a little more juice flowing.

HELEN: They were B.

BOB: They spent less time worrying about makeup than worrying about their cashmere sweater collection.

HELEN: They were more real. It's true. It's disgusting, all this. And then there were a whole slew of other clubs, so if you were acned, you could belong to the acne club...if you were convex, whatever.

BOB: The top of the pecking order was the Tantras.

HELEN: Just a minute. Are *you* supposed to be reporting on club order?

BOB: I married a Tantra. I am an expert.

HELEN: There was a song, "A Man Without a Tantra." [sings]:

A man without a Tantra is like a ship without a sail
It's like a boat without a rudder, it's like a kite without a tail, without a tail;
A man without a Tantra is the saddest thing I know
Because there's one thing worse in this universe
And that's a Tantra, I mean a Tantra, I said a Tantra without a man.
Now you can roll a silver dollar down a ballroom floor
And it'll roll 'cause it's round
A Tantra doesn't know what a good man she's got
Until she's turned him down.
So listen, honey, listen to me because I want you to understand
That as a silver dollar goes from hand to hand
A Tantra goes from man to man. I really mean it.
A Tantra goes from man to man. Except on Sundays!
A Tantra goes from man to man.

BOB: Absurd, "except on Sundays." This is a Jewish club! And they didn't go from man to man.

HELEN: I thought we were all virgins.

BOB: They were all virgins. You can see why I couldn't relate to these people. When did you sing that song?

HELEN: All the time. I mean how would I know it if we didn't sing it all the time? And the Barons had a song.

BOB: No, the boys just talked about if they could go out with a girl and feel her up. That was a big deal. Everybody was really horny. With no birth control but condoms, and we carried them around all the time. Boys carried condoms around, but if you ever got lucky, probably the condom was already three years old and had deteriorated, right?

HELEN: You could have your choice, though, of clubs; there were pretty much clubs for everybody. You would have to rush to join.

BOB: They divided everyone up for the rush period. You didn't sign up when you registered for school.

HELEN: They invited you--I think that the girls who belonged to the clubs would just kind of call you up on the phone and talk to you. And they didn't want to give you two invitations. So I was rushed by Donatellos and Tantras. And those were the only clubs that I was interested in. And my cousin was a Donatello, and we never spoke very much, but I remember her calling me. They made her call me and make up with me so that I would join their club. I didn't even know we were mad at one another!

BOB: Helen was a social hot dog in ninth grade and had a strong circle of friends. Where I was a social isolate.

HELEN: But I was always different. I was not a follower. Strangely enough, I decided to join when I was in junior high school. One of my best friends chose Donatellos. And I became a Tantra. One of the club members just called you up and talked to you. I thought the Tantras were nicer, that I had more in common with the Tantras.

BOB: When you were in the club, over the next three years, were you ever rush chair? Who was in charge of hustling the kids coming up from junior high school?

HELEN: I don't think we had a rush chair. We had a club president. I can't remember who was in charge of new members. There was a hierarchy. They would make up what to do with rush. You just *became* a Tantra; they didn't boss you around. If they did haze, it was totally nontraumatic, because I can't remember anything.

BOB: At the boys' clubs, they put all the boys through hazing rituals.

HELEN: If they did it with us it was just very minor. But people were probably afraid of me, so they probably didn't make me do anything. I am--was-- standoffish. We had an initiation luncheon once a year, or once a semester, where they would give you something that made you a Tantra. They would give you a flower, name you a flower. I was a daffodil. And they gave me a poem. My big sister gave me a poem which said, "Daffodils come in the spring, 'tis true; but here's one that's with us the whole year through. Helen's a girl who's lots of fun, and--" I don't remember the rest. But I was a daffodil and I was thinking, what a dopey flower that is. *Now* I think it's beautiful, but then, I was thinking I didn't like yellow, it was a pretty dopey flower, and I didn't much like it.

BOB: Your big sister was in my class. I never dated these girls; I don't think I said three words to them in three years!

HELEN: I didn't like being a daffodil. That's all I can remember.   We had dances. I was once in a fashion show, at a department store, where I won "Model of the Day." I was representing the Tantras because the real model--she was a tall, thin, gorgeous woman--was sick. There were fashion shows, socials with other clubs--

BOB: And the girls would wear a lot of makeup. They would sort of be competitive to see who could be the most mature; i.e., like their mothers! And they smoked cigarettes.

HELEN: We smoked during our meetings. We had meetings. We sat around in a circle. Every once in a while we'd play "Truth." We'd say things to hurt people's feelings. But I never cried at a meeting because I think I was only half there. We'd talk about who we were bringing into our club and we'd plan our Tantra dance, our Baron/Tantra dance; we had dances with the Barons. The dances were at places like Sportsman's, and you had to pay to get in.

BOB: The purpose of these clubs was to keep people's minds off sex. The dances were expensive. You'd have to buy tickets, and the dances cost like seven dollars. I used to go out with girls from L.A. High, Hollywood High, Hamilton High, and Beverly High; I never went out with girls from Fairfax.

HELEN: Our schools hardly ever had dances. If they did none of us would attend; only the nonclub people went. You didn't have to go to school dances because the Barons and Tantras had them, or the Cardinals and Donatellos had them.

BOB: This was a different era. If a guy took a girl out on a date, in high school, on a Saturday night, he'd wear a tie. We used to wear ties to go out on a date. The other thing was, we're talking car culture. This was L.A., and there were drive-ins. Many more drive-ins than we have now. And certain clubs sort of had drive-ins where they hung out and people would cruise. There was a drive-in on Beverly and LaBrea that's gone. There was a drive-in on Pico near Fairfax. There was Delores Drive-in, which was very famous, one of the last of the drive-ins in L.A., that was near LaCienega and Wilshire. There was another drive-in in downtown Beverly Hills, where the Beverly Hills kids used to hang out. And so part of the social life also revolved around drive-ins. During the week! And week nights!

HELEN: We all would go to Delores's. Ah, Delores's was cool. You know all of the drive-ins that they show in these old movies? Like *American Graffiti?* They're all replicas of Delores's. You would get hamburgers and vanilla Cokes. It was just Coke with vanilla at the bottom, but--

BOB: That was a big thing in the drugstores, getting Coca-Cola with a squirt of some kind of syrup in it. Some flavor.

HELEN: You had these trays that you could fit on your door, or the driving wheel.

BOB: And your carhop would come and deliver the food to you. There was another drive-in at Sunset and LaBrea. There were five or six in the Hollywood/Beverly Hills area.

HELEN: The Tantras and the guys hung out at the Delores Drive-In. You could also go inside if you wanted. That was the place to be. I can remember driving there. My sister got married and she left me her car, which had a stickshift. I drove that car and I could hardly shift. It took me five minutes to put it in reverse and another five to put it into first. But you'd always be able to find somebody you knew, and somebody to hang out with, at Delores's. And see what was happening.

BOB: And these drive-ins were a little bit of contrast to other famous drive-ins in L.A., like Bob's Big Boy in Van Nuys. That was different. More of a low-rider hot-rod type deal, out in the Valley. Kids were very status-conscious about cars.

HELEN: I think *American Graffiti* really sums up Delores's Drive-In. When I watch that movie and that drive-in I just flip right back to it.

BOB: Well, that was filmed in Modesto. But it was fifties culture. It was universal. Even L.A. was a "small town" then.

HELEN: Then eventually they evolved into where you could give your order in the stand and they'd come and bring it out to you. They had a speaker, a labor-saving device. Like Jack-in-the-Box now.

BOB: They had male car-hops at Delores. Remember that?

HELEN: I never made friends with any car-hops. I was too busy looking for guys.

BOB: Delores is very famous. When Delores closed and they put up an office building there, it was written up in the L.A. Times. Because it was like a monument.

HELEN: Delores's was *it* for the kids I knew. My life, growing up--I didn't know any of those guys who were in fights. I had a very different experience in high school.   My sister was older and she used to bring guys over to our house. And then I had guys who were good friends of mine. And they would all come over. My house was kind of "open house" all the time! Lots of club guys. It was great fun.

BOB: If you didn't go to Delores's, or to a drive-in, you went out for coffee because it was a cheap date. But what was interesting was that gasoline was real cheap in those days, twenty-five a gallon. We would jump in the car and drive to Palm Springs for coffee. That's 120 miles! People would do that sort of thing. It was a way of being alone with somebody, but it wasn't sexual. Here you're in the car, you're going someplace, you're moving, da da da. You can be *with* somebody privately. Then there was Easter in Palm Springs, which has become such a big deal that it's totally out of hand, but we had our own version of that in the fifties where kids would go to Palm Springs and twelve people would sleep in a room with two beds. No sex! No sex. It was just being there, and hanging out.

HELEN: Sure, the Tantras went over Easter break. All of us. We shared a room, we sat in the sun, we walked, we talked to boys and flirted and kissed--

BOB: --now and then, and went home! The other thing was beach dates in the summertime. Will Rogers State Beach. And there were two or three beaches between there and Santa Monica Pier. Roadside. Muscle Beach. Agony Hollow. These were beaches where people went to hang out. And there were people there who were in college at UCLA or USC. Roadside was where Fairfax guys went for crap games.

HELEN: *I* went to summer school.

BOB: There was another pervasive phenomenon in the fifties at Fairfax High School, and that was gambling. Crap games after school.

HELEN: We never did that; they'd come over to our house and we'd dance, talk, and eat. I had a very positive experience in high school. Most of the guys I knew were older and in Bob's class. When we went to his reunion I knew as many people in his class as he did. I didn't have as much fun at my reunion, because I never hung out with the girls. I hung out with the guys in his class.
    I *had* a boyfriend, and so these guys were just friends. I met my boyfriend when I was fifteen. And we were boyfriend and girlfriend all through high school. I always had a date for Saturday night. That was a *big deal,* to have a date for Saturday night. I always did. I'd have a date Friday night, too!

BOB: The guys I hung out with rarely had dates. And they were in clubs, all of the guys that I hung out with. The primary reason guys would try to get a date with a girl was you thought that you could have some kind of sexual conquest. Probably very modest, but--

HELEN: I did not know Bob in high school. We were there, though, at the same time. He married two Tantras and I married two guys who were never in clubs!

BOB: Oh. The dances. I don't recall ever going to a Fairfax dance. A boy's club and a girls' club would get together and have an annual dance. And then they'd have to hustle tickets to recoup the cost of the hall, the band, the promotion. Now I never went to dances at Fairfax, but I went to a few at Hamilton High. You put on a dark suit, you bought a corsage, like you were going to a wedding! This was a big deal! And there was a lot of making out. There was a lot of swapping spit, with girls. But the corsage, the tie, it was very inhibiting. It was horrible. It was a terrible time to have raging hormones, I'll tell you.

HELEN: It wasn't inhibiting to everyone. My high school years were a lot of fun. Bob's were hateful. I mean that he says he hated his.

BOB: I was depressed.

HELEN: And I wasn't! I was a normal kid. Now, for these dances, we hired bands, and they played jitterbug and slow dances.

BOB: All those sappy songs. The stuff that was on the charts at the time.

HELEN: The first song I can remember was Johnny Ray, singing "The Little White Cloud That Cried."

BOB: Lots of maudlin, treacley love songs.

HELEN: I remember that a group of us danced to "Shboom" for the last assembly at Fairfax when we graduated. We made up a song for our senior whatever it was, finale.

BOB: I don't think I was particularly typical in high school because I used to listen to the jazz station in town, which was a very weak station out of Long Beach, with a disc jockey at night by the name of Sleepy Stein. I never listened to the AM stations. It was the beginning of rock and roll. And there was a white disc jockey in town by the name of Huggy Boy and this was when the onebutton roll suit came in, the long jacket, kind of funny-looking pants, blue suede shoes. I used to go down to rock and roll concerts with black musicians, mostly, at the Shrine Auditorium, and there wouldn't be very many white people, and--

HELEN: No one I knew did that! He was always exotic.

BOB: There used to be, down at the corner of Central Avenue and Vernon--a black neighborhood--there was a very large black record store called "Dolphin's of Hollywood." This is like fifteen miles from Hollywood. Right? Dolphin's of Hollywood was like a big black record store and I would go down there and listen to records. And it was sort of the heart of it all, if you wanted to buy black music records.

HELEN: *Nobody,* there was nobody I knew who wanted to do that at Fairfax besides you. No wonder you didn't have any friends!

BOB: And I listened to Hunter Hancock. You bet.

HELEN: I never dated non-Jewish guys in high school at all. There were like no non-Jewish guys at Fairfax. Well, there might have been one or two non-Jewish guys.

BOB: There was more than one; there was Roger. And what about Al Radford and his brother Bo?
    The basic thing was if you went steady with somebody and you had a long-term relationship, which was like four or five or six months or more, then it was okay to have sex.

HELEN: That must be your *fantasy! I* had plenty of friends, and we all went out all through high school, and *none* of us did it--ah, I don't think.

BOB: Primarily it was just like you'd expect in any relationship--if they're together, they're together! They're going to get it on!

HELEN: He's absolutely wrong. He is absolutely 100 percent wrong.

BOB: No, no, no. I'm not saying that every couple did it. What I'm saying is that if a couple was going together they had a sexual relationship. Of sorts: now, whether guys were *penetrating* girls or not, I don't know. There were a lot of girls doing oral sex.

HELEN: No! No! *Wrong.*

BOB: You didn't take out girls, so you didn't know.

HELEN: You didn't take out one girl from Fairfax by your own admission. So be quiet.

BOB: I took out girls from Hamilton and L.A. High--

HELEN: *Everybody* at Hamilton did it! Everybody knows that the whole *school* did it. Fairfax was different because we were Jewish.

BOB: You can see why I didn't waste my time with these girls at Fairfax High School.

HELEN: Maybe the Zephs did it.

BOB: All of those schools were predominantly Jewish.

HELEN: But Doing It: we would talk about our own personal decisions, and we would--you'd have your little cliques where you would talk about everything. Sex wasn't a big topic.

BOB: I had friends like that one girl, you remember her--

HELEN: She was in my club. I know she didn't do it. *She was a Tantra!*

BOB: So girls weren't considered sluts if they had sex with a guy who was their boyfriend?

HELEN: They were considered "racy." There was one girl who believed in "free love."

BOB: Because she was having sex with her boyfriend--

HELEN: Who she married--

BOB: They became boyfriend and girlfriend when they were fourteen! And they're still together. Helen thinks that there was no sex before 1970. Are you out of your gourd?

HELEN: I thought I knew everything because I was a Tantra.

BOB: But there was another phenomenon at the high school that was very profound, and this was Fairfax High School, Beverly, and Hollywood. Some of the girls that were particularly attractive and looked "mature" sometimes dated guys that were six, seven, eight years older. Seventeen-year-old gals would be dating guys in their early twenties. So part of this whole bit was the hairdos and the makeup and the cigarette and the cashmere sweaters, trying to look like their mothers, seventeen years old, dating guys who were seniors at UCLA or law students. I mean, I even took out girls from high school when I was a freshman or sophomore in college. A lot of us took out younger girls. Now. *These* boys, by the time they were in college, were a little more sophisticated with girls than high school boys were. They had a better chance of consummating a relationship. There was that element going on as well. And the boys used to talk in high school about the girls who were dating guys from college, assuming that they were sleeping with them.

HELEN: When we went to our high school reunion and looked at the couples there, some of them were high school sweethearts. Some of them were still together.

BOB: Who knows if it worked out? But girls didn't have many options. You could be a teacher or a nurse. And boys could be engineers, doctors, and lawyers.

HELEN: I had a good time. But it wasn't the Tantras that made the good time. If I wasn't in the Tantras I wouldn't have had *as good a time* because I would have had the stigma of not being accepted by the pretty girls. And that would have meant that I wasn't pretty and that would have been some outside recognition that I wasn't as pretty as those girls. Once I was accepted, I didn't pay much attention to them! Now, about the clubs at L.A. High: you knew who were the better ones, who were the worse ones. I think the Baronettes and Sans Souci and Vogue at L.A. High were like the Donatellos and Tantras at Fairfax.

BOB: I went out with L.A. High girls in Sans Souci. I dated this girl who had this enormous bosom. And I looked like I was about eleven years old. And she had these enormous breasts and the closest I ever got to them was when she was sitting next to me in the movie and I looked so young it was like she was with her kid brother! High school, God, it was horrible.

HELEN: I wasn't sad when I graduated. Because I was going to go on to college. It was exciting for me. High school and the rules there were so nontraumatic for me. I wasn't a rebel; I conformed as much as I had to conform; it was just an *American Graffiti* kind of experience.

BOB: With guys, wearing Levis or chinos with tennis shoes to school, it wasn't a lot different than it is today. Girls couldn't wear Levis. No pants. But here's the racy stuff, with certain girls at Fairfax High. They'd have a perfume bottle. Only it wouldn't have perfume in it. They'd have gin. Or vodka.

HELEN: *Girls?* This is what the nonaffiliated *boys* did.

BOB: I'm not saying every girl! There was the *occasional* girl who had a little bottle of vodka. This was radical.

HELEN: I never knew anybody like that. Ever. I never talked to anybody like that. Like that girl who was the school "slut"--

BOB: Forget about her; I liked her. She was in my class, too.

HELEN: She was called "All the Way." She once gave the whole damn football team crabs. And I know this because I had home room with the idiot coach and he told us all about the problem!

BOB: She did not sleep with whole *groups* of guys!
   The thing about Fairfax that was very strong was there was a lot of respect for people who did well in school and were academically oriented: all those guys who wanted to be doctors and lawyers. Those guys *studied*. They didn't just party. They *studied*. And there were a lot of guys in clubs who went on to excel in school. And there was the Ephebian Society, all the people who had the respect of the faculty. And they weren't all nerds. They did the school paper, student government, that stuff. And that was cool. Not everybody was a party animal. Nothing like that. There was a pecking order, but--

HELEN: It certainly wasn't like it is today, and it wasn't like Beverly High or the private schools at that time--

BOB: Fairfax was almost an all-Jewish high school and had the highest percentage of its graduating classes go on to four-year schools of any school in the city. The chemistry kids won the American Chemical Society scholastic competition between the high schools; we had this real hot chemistry teacher, Mr. Toon. They had good English classes. There was a very strong scholastic element in that school. Education was important. So it wasn't just all this frivolous club shit with sweaters and jackets. I mean that was there, but the school did what it was supposed to do. And the streets were safe in those days. And Jack Kemp was the quarterback when I was in the tenth grade. We had good "B" football league teams, for smaller guys. We never had big linemen for the varsity.

HELEN: Fairfax was interesting. There was a lot of homogeneity. You felt like you were part of one big family.

BOB: The school was very conscious that it was primarily Jewish and had a sense of humor about it, you bet. But the other schools were anti-Semitic. Hollywood High: no Jews there; very few. But a lot of anti-Semitism. You know, I could have gone to Hollywood High.

HELEN: I could have, too, but I had no desire to. I went to summer school at Hollywood one year and I enjoyed it because it was so much easier than Fairfax.

When I left Fairfax, the first summer after I graduated, I went to L.A. City College. It was incredible; it was like being back in high school. It was much easier than Fairfax High School. So while I didn't study much, the level of education at Fairfax was superior. It prepared you for college.

BOB: I had a girlfriend who went to Beverly High. And she occasionally passed off an old English paper from Beverly High at UCLA, and she got a better grade at UCLA than at Beverly High! And UCLA was a first-class school with a rigorous English Department. Our high schools were good high schools!

HELEN: But for girls--I took one class, before I graduated, on buying groceries or something, home preparation, how to write a check--Home Ec. It was totally useless. This wasn't cooking. It was supposed to have something to do with "life preparation." Very rudimentary: I thought it was the stupidest class I'd ever seen. But I wasn't rebellious--I was a kid. Girls did girl things and boys did boy things. In junior high school we took Home Ec and the boys took Shop, either Wood Shop or Print Shop. We had to take Home Ec; we had to take that stupid sewing class, too--where you had to embroider your name on your gym blouse.

BOB: I took Wood Shop in junior high school and I was totally incompetent. The first exercise in woodshop was to make a broom holder, shaped like this, to put in your closet so a broom could stand up, like this. And of course that's a three-day project. It took me *sixteen weeks!*

HELEN: He's really very talented, my husband. But he doesn't seem to be able to *make* things, or *fix* things. He breaks them, like a bull in a china shop.

BOB: I thought, what am I doing here? I want to go out and read a Russian novel! What is this shit with the *broom holder?*

HELEN: So they started pretty early, with the boy/girl things. Now, in gym, we wore black gym shorts and they had snaps on the sides. Short, white blouse, V-neck, with a pocket and your name embroidered on that. White socks. White shoes. And nobody, *nobody,* wanted to take a shower after gym. Nobody, even though you were supposed to. We got out of showering as much as we could. I hated taking showers there; you'd mess your hair up. And we tried to get out of gym; my sister had ingenious ways. She had her period every day, for instance.

BOB: I always played sports. Five out of six semesters, I went out for sports. We had gym sixth period and we stayed and worked out. But I never knew what after-school culture was because I was always on the sports field! What did kids do at three o'clock?

HELEN: Walk home. Do homework. Talk on the phone. And then the guys would start coming by. Now, I played basketball and baseball in school, but not competitively. Oh, and we had those stupid jumping jacks. I really hated them. We had to do five million of them, and then we'd run and throw.

BOB: I don't recall ever seeing girls play basketball when I was a kid.

HELEN: We played basketball. Volleyball, we played. Basketball was half court: you could only take three steps, or it would be too "strenuous." We didn't have track, as far as I can recall.

BOB: I don't remember any girls' sports teams at Fairfax. *Ever.*

HELEN: There weren't sports teams; this is what we played during gym.

BOB: There was a very tacky girls' gym that was grossly inadequate. The boys' gym was inadequate, too. We were mostly outside. And we ate outside. *No one* ever ate in the cafeteria. I don't think I was in there once in three years. The way the school was configured, like, there was a cafeteria I never went into, but there was a little fast-food window, and you'd stand in line to buy stuff. And the club kids had their own tables that really were the turf of the club. The kids in the clubs would congregate at their tables. And so they had their own turf at the morning recess and at the lunch hour. Wasn't there like a ten-minute break in the morning? And so the kids in the clubs would go out and then they'd congregate at their tables. *They had a place to go.* That was one of the manifestations of the clubs. It was not only if they had a jacket or a sweater, but that they had a place where they congregated. And clubs tended to cluster.

HELEN: He's absolutely right. And at lunchtime, we used to go out on the front lawn and eat lunch on the grass. We had our own circles. The Tantras were *here,* the Donatellos were *there.* Guys would come from L.A. High to see their girlfriends--that kind of stuff.

BOB: It was a no-no to leave and go to other campuses. But I did it. Now, people were friendly. It wasn't like a We/They situation. It wasn't rigid. It was a mind-set: club/nonclub.

HELEN: It was a place to belong.

BOB: People who weren't in clubs could hang out. I would have lunch with friends of mine. And be with the guys. It wasn't a big deal.

HELEN: The school would play music on the loudspeakers. We'd always have some rock and roll over the speakers.

BOB: The speakers! There were also morning announcements. Korean War, Eisenhower. Those were the days when there was a Cold War and we all believed America was invincible. And always right.

HELEN: Well, we are. We were. Weren't we, then?

BOB: And then the Korean War came and MacArthur got his ass kicked. And people thought that was an anomaly, some kind of fuck-up. "The Communists *made* us do not as well as we should have." Et cetera, et cetera. We believed all that bullshit about our bombers that could go anywhere. It was good guys and bad guys. I mean this is forty years ago. This is ancient history.

HELEN: Here's our Colonial Yearbook. This guy died. He died, too. She's still beautiful; she was a *Tantra*. See, now, there *were* girls in ROTC. And they were popular girls, look, they were Donatellos.

BOB: This guy killed himself. He was a great baseball player. His major league baseball career as a lefty with the Chicago White Sox ended when he was in his early twenties. And he came back to L.A. and he was depressed. I don't know the story. But he wound up going to the mound at the high school, on the weekend, and there he shot himself in the head. It's like fiction. But it was real. And I knew him.

6

The Intermarriage of
Myra and Roger

"Are you out of your minds?"
"How will you raise the children?"
"Who will your friends be, socially?"
"And who could you get to perform the ceremony?"

These were among the questions Myra and Roger entertained as they announced their
intention to build a life together in the late 1950s. High school, with its elaborate systems
of ethnic and gender segregation, its emphasis on the perils of sexuality, had failed to
obstruct the love affair of a Jew and a Gentile.

By 1959, the citizens of the United States were no longer shielded from bearing
witness to attempted desegregation in the South. Television, radio, and newspapers
broadcast responses to the recent Supreme Court decision on *Brown v. the Board of
Education* and covered the 1955 Montgomery, Alabama, bus boycott initiated by Rosa
Parks's refusal to give her seat to a white man. By 1956, federal troops had to be sent
to enforce the federally mandated integration of Central High School in Little Rock,
Arkansas. The emergence of Dr. Martin Luther King, Jr., as a leader in Alabama's black
community [and beyond] paralleled the swift politicization of both black and white high
school students across the South. For frightened white supremacists, the spectre of
"miscegenation," or interracial sex, marriage, and childbearing, was the final taboo--a
spectre effectively invoked by the Ku Klux Klan and myriad white power groups as a
warning light against the integration of young people.

Considering this powerful backdrop, it would be historically and politically inaccurate
to compare the intermarriage of Jew and Gentile in Los Angeles to a black/white union
in any region of the United States that same year. Furthermore, the Jews' experience of
ethnic discrimination in America did not prevent their own stereotyping of black and
Hispanic Americans as "other"; racism within the Jewish community--and black anti-
Semitism in turn--are painful topics commanding ongoing examination and dialogue
today. What is significant to this story is that the white power literature of the 1950s,

with its incendiary rhetoric on the evils of racemixing, *consistently* included attacks on Jewish influence, and in this cultural race war Jews were not counted as white. In many minds, Roger and Myra's intermarriage was very controversial.

Because nice Jewish girls were supposed to marry nice Jewish boys, Myra acquired a cachet of radicalism, which in her case was never political. She simply loved Roger. It was, ironically, their intention to legitimize this love through traditional matrimony which stunned their critics. Nonetheless, wedding plans proceeded, and, ultimately without boycott, the ceremony took place at the Bel Air Hotel in February of 1959. A gracious gesture of blessing for the newlyweds arrived in the form of a silver shot glass, sent by the Academy Awardwinning actress Greer Garson, who had employed Myra as her private secretary during the previous year.

This interview began during a family vacation at the beach, appropriately enough, in an environment similar to that of Myra and Roger's 1955 courtship.

MYRA: Opposites attracted. In high school, the group that I liked were almost always guys who were part of a faster crowd, who were good-looking, and who were exciting to me. The Jewish boys I knew were nice guys, studious, sober, and responsible, but I found that I wanted excitement, too. I'm sorry, but it was true. So I married your father instead.

Roger's different life was exciting to me,--in the same way that one might be interested in people from other cultures, other countries. Somebody else's world is mysterious; it's intriguing, especially when you know that your parents and all your relatives are saying, "No. No. No. Wrong. Danger. You stay over here *inside this corral. This* is good, *this* is safe. We love you and we want to protect you, don't go over there, you're going to regret it. Eventually it's going to come to no good no matter how nice the boy is; you're going to 'get into trouble', or your heart will be broken." That was always said! My grandmother told me the *goyim* were all snobs. And I heard at home that eventually "they" would turn on you, no matter how good your friendship was. Obviously, I was tempted! I wanted to see! To try!

School activities were kind of interesting and fun and attracted the part of me that was idealistic and democratic. Despite all the bullshit stuff about rules, I had a real desire to do some service and liked the fact that the service organizations were supposedly open to everybody: blacks, Chinese. We *didn't* mix socially. And the social institutions of fraternities and sororities, known as clubs, were supported fully by the school administration. They supplied the rush lists from which the clubs invited you to teas. And those rush lists were for white and/or Jewish students only. Now, were there separate clubs for black or Asian students? You know, I have *no idea*.

At L.A. High it was almost all white. But during our time, they closed some other school and new kids came to L.A. High; then the makeup of the school changed markedly, in my senior year. The sororities went way back, many years. And the girls' vice-principal would supply a list of Jews and Gentiles to the clubs. If you were Jewish, you were just not *invited* to the Gentile rush teas. They knew who was who. Now, there were a few people of mixed parentage--they might have been invited to both, but typically, you would tend to hang out with *either* Jewish *or* non-Jewish girls, and then be invited to that bunch of clubs.

I met Roger when I was in my senior year, just before my last semester of high school. We went out for three years, but I decided we were going to get married after about three weeks. When did you decide, Rog?

ROGER: About three years.

MYRA: It's true. He didn't phrase it that way. It was more like, if he were through with school, and independent, and, and--

ROGER: It finally dawned on me that I wasn't going to break up with Myra.

MYRA: He has such a romantic way of putting it.

ROGER: No, what I mean is we were going to stay together.

MYRA: Sort of like I'm a *leech,* that's the way it sounds.

ROGER: In those days, you either split or you got married. In other words, the alternative of just hanging with each other wasn't available. Oh, it was *available* but--

MYRA: --we didn't think about it. Now, one of my friends did a very far-out thing for that time: she left home and went and lived with a guy, while we were still in college. Nobody did that!

ROGER: Well, you *could* do it. Myra just told you that some did. But it would cause *so much trouble* in your respective families!

MYRA: You'd make a break with your families if you did that. That was it!

ROGER: You'd have to leave your family; you'd have to say good-bye to your parents. And unless you had a terrible home life, as some people did, you didn't want to do that. There wasn't a real option. There were too many complications, too many lifted eyebrows. Hell, just an interreligious marriage lifted eyebrows all over the place at that time. Can you imagine what living together would do?

Once we had made clear our good intentions--well, then we just floated. But still had to confront a lot of peoples' reactions about the religious difference. *Every* person, in fact.

MYRA: *Every single person* thought they had the right--

ROGER: Everybody and their uncle gave us advice.

MYRA: They mostly asked questions. *"How are you going to raise the children?"*

ROGER: *"How are you going to raise the children?"* was question number one. And question number two was, well, *"How are you going to work it out?"* And my answer was: "There isn't anything to work out! I'm not religious. Myra's not particularly religious. There's nothing to work out. We don't have any problem!" And then they would immediately say, especially if they were an adult, "No, no, that's not what I'm talking about. I'm talking about the *social implications.* Who are you going to hang out with? Who are your friends going to be? What is going to be your center of identification? Look about you. Note that the Jewish community is separate from the non-Jewish community, and that's separate from the black community, and that's separate from the Japanese community. And that's separate from the Mexican community. That's the way society is organized! Now, you have a mixed marriage. Who are *you* going to hang out with?" It wasn't quite put that way, but that was the question. That was the question. And it was a legit question at that time. And still is today, to a lesser extent.

But we were smarter than they were; more optimistic, I should say. Because we, having grown up in another generation--the next generation--saw that it was possible. I was a non-Jewish guy in an all-Jewish club. I had no problems. We made millions of jokes about it, okay? And I was in there joking right along with everyone. But there was no problem! I knew Yiddish words, idioms, jokes.

MYRA: Pat told me that *all* of her friends were Jewish until she got to L.A. High. And then, because of the institutionalized clubs, she had to hang out with kids who were not Jews.

Now, the *real* first question amongst all our friends and acquaintances, which was not spoken directly, was "Are you sleeping together?" That was numero uno. It amused me that everybody was wondering. I didn't have to say anything because the question was never put to me directly! But we knew they all wanted to know. The thing is, I came from a background of very sober, responsible kinds of good-girl behavior, and Roger was known as being very fast. He didn't take out girls that didn't put out. And so what was going on here? We have these two extremes who are suddenly together! So they must be getting it on; otherwise he wouldn't be taking her out. He would never have taken her out a second time. So, we kept them all guessing, which was kind of fun. But I was so much more consumed with the *agony* of our relationship--you know, being *in love*--that I didn't have time to enjoy that until the last year.

ROGER: The last year, things settled down. After about two years of going together we finally said, okay, I'm going to finish school and get my degree and get a job someplace, and we're going to get married when I finish college. No point in getting married until I get out of college, because I can't support us.

MYRA: I lived at home until I married. I never even went away to camp! I was really unusual, a real throwback. I was very uncomfortable and timid about new situations. Yet I had planned to go away to college, to go to Berkeley, before I met Roger.

ROGER: Hell, she won every award they had. She could have gone to any school she wanted. She probably could have gone to Harvard!

MYRA: No. I didn't want to. I wanted to be where Roger was. And preparing to marry was fun. I was very happy and excited about getting married. I didn't feel fearful at all.

ROGER: Because it was normal. We went through the normal drill.

MYRA: I mean, I was in love! I was crazy in love! I was happy! I had just what I wanted. It was wonderful! And I had a beautiful wedding. My family was happy. They liked Rog. My mother really had gotten to know him. My father, I don't know what my father was thinking. By the time we were getting married there was no talking us out of it because we had been going together for three and a half years. Everyone, whether happily or not, had accepted the fact that this was it. We were getting married. Period. I didn't have any firm ideas about how we were going to "raise the kids"; not really. I was more concerned that we were going to play house for a while.

ROGER: I had very definite ideas. The first was that the kids were not going to be sent to Sunday School or to be given a selected religion. We were going to *discuss* religion, be aware of the fact that there *was* religion, and be aware of background, but no forced, given identification. That was one. The second rule I had was that the kids were going to enjoy the same standard of living that we had: no more, no less. Many parents tried to give their kids a standard of living *they* couldn't afford. The kids felt uncomfortable and guilty about their parents' sacrifices. And the result was, consistently, that the kids resented their parents for it. For example, the family who lived in back of us sent their kids to private military school, and the kids were just juvenile delinquents. Hell's Angels. Okay? And there was another example--

MYRA: Somebody your mother worked with. She was a single woman, and she had her kid in private school; she was trying to give him all the advantages, and he was hating her. Because he didn't have the background all the other kids did, and felt out of his league at school.

ROGER: See? And so early on, I formed the attitude that I wasn't going to play that game. Our kids would enjoy the same standard of living that we did. *We* weren't immigrants. We didn't have to live for our kids, to enjoy success vicariously because we had accents, or any of that sort of thing. I fully intended to live well and to have fun and to enjoy life, and the kids could live well and have fun and enjoy life just like me. But not more than me.

MYRA: He had strong opinions about a lot of things. I was a very unformed, embryonic personality. I really was! I didn't know who I was or where I was going. I wanted to please the people I cared about. So I would have done whatever he wanted me to do. If he had wanted me to become Catholic, or a Methodist, I would have done that.

ROGER: Well, we were Unitarians for a little while, but that didn't last very long.

MYRA: You just didn't question it: you did what your husband or boyfriend wanted you to do. That's just the way it was--straight out of the Bible. Ruth said, "Thy people shall be my people!"
    Also, like most children of immigrants I got a strong message to assimilate. I would have gladly gone all the way with that, but the more I assimilated the more friction it created at home. Every immigrant family faces the same dilemma. They want their kids to have open doors and free choices and yet somehow retain their ethnic or cultural identity. I'm being perfectly honest. I wanted to be accepted by the great "middle majority," which was so interesting to me because it *was* so different--and safe. It was a social thing, not a religious thing. For me.

ROGER: Interesting. You see, Myra grew up--

MYRA: Wait. Let me articulate it first and then you can comment on how you perceived it. I thought that my Gentile friends had wilder, freer lives than I did. The Jews at that time were very, understandably, cautious. I came from East European Jewish immigrants: my grandmother, who came here from Warsaw as an adult; my mother, who immigrated with her as a child. Yeah. And I learned from them that being Jewish was a heavy burden. But I was young and didn't want to carry that burden.
    And yet, I have always loved my Jewish relatives, and I got along very well with everybody. In their safe, warm company, being Jewish was comfortable. So, I was a chameleon. I also think that there is, for everybody, a certain amount of questioning what your parents have given you. *And this was my way*

of rebelling. So that's tied up in there too.

There were different socioeconomic groups of Jewish kids. I grew up with kids who were comfortable, middle-class, but not rich. Most of the girls who became Dantes, or Tantras, had more money than I did. A lot was decided along money lines; what kind of clothes you wore to high school determined, to some extent, what club you got into. Isn't that true, Rog?

I had nice clothes, a *few* things that were great. But I wasn't that hung up about clothes. I wasn't very *acquisitive;* money wasn't an issue for me. However, other people saw money as a potential problem in our marriage. There was very much of an upwardly mobile attitude amongst the Jewish kids I grew up with. At Fairfax and L.A. High, the kids were all going to make it, all going to make it.

ROGER: Now, *that's* the point I was going to raise a while back.

MYRA: *I* didn't care that much! I wanted to live happily ever after and play house with Roger. It would be fine if we were going to be middle, middle majority Gentile people without a lot of income. I don't think money was a serious issue with us.

ROGER: Money is always an issue. Society is, was, and always will be divided up into various socioeconomic classes, not independent of ethnicity but cross-ethnic. In high school you got a kind of fuzzy understanding of that, but it became particularly intense in the twelfth grade and later, because there were two major dividing lines that occurred around twelfth grade. The first dividing line was between the kids that went to college and the kids that didn't go to college. All right? And that was very serious. That was a *big* divider. However, there was an escape valve. There were kids who didn't go to college but went into their parents' business. Okay? Boys. Like that guy whose father owned a chicken store--

MYRA: I never considered not going to college.

ROGER: Among girls, the Jewish girls, you either went to college or you got married.

MYRA: Or you became a dental assistant. Being a dental assistant was the third choice among the girls in my club. I'm not kidding!

ROGER: There was a middle-class attitude that was absolutely shunned by the upwardly mobile Jewish kids at Fairfax and L.A. High. That's what you didn't want to know from, the trap you wanted to escape. The idea was that life on a middle-class income was dreary and déclassé.

MYRA: I didn't think it was, as long as you weren't Jewish. Somehow romantic love and acceptance would compensate for any economic deprivation.

ROGER: The concern over money in a mixed marriage wasn't specifically expressed, but it was there, big time. First, there was the Jewish upward mobility we've already mentioned. Second, women were dependent on their husbands for their comfort and status. Third, Gentiles were perceived by Jews as less reliable family men--drinking, carousing. Fourth, Gentile women were perceived as meek and mild--less demanding. All this led to the stereotype that a mixed marriage had a much better chance if the man was Jewish and the woman Gentile. We were doing the opposite--danger!

MYRA: The Jews had a large network of relatives and friends who helped each other. Like other immigrant groups: Asians and Italians have done the same.

ROGER: The Jews not only knew people who were big time in the entertainment business and commerce, but who were professional men--doctors, lawyers.

MYRA: And the doctors were all Top Men in Their Field. Always! At least it seemed like nobody ever went to a doctor who was not a Top Man in His Field. He was always somebody's brother-in-law or cousin. In the network people did favors for one another. If you needed something there was always a *mayven,* an expert, you could rely upon, usually a relative or friend. If you were in the manufacturing business, like my father--and my father was a very respected and ethical man--a friend could come to you and buy something wholesale, and he would return the favor. No one kept records of the sales. Cash sales, they were called. "I can get it for you wholesale" is now an American cliché.

ROGER: So the problem for us in the late 1950s was really what camp to buy into.

MYRA: Still is. We have our own camp.

ROGER: There were a bunch of them, and they were graded. And the camp that was attractive to a group of Jewish kids in high school and college, too, in our time, was yuppie. They wanted to be yuppies. The word wasn't coined yet, but that's what they wanted to be. They wanted *respect.* And the idea of how to get respect was to have money, clothes, cars, go out to dinner at fancy places, participate.

MYRA: To know what's happening: not to be uncool.

ROGER: Yeah, to have knowledgeable and wealthy friends whose achievements matched your own, and to generally exist in the comfortable and knowledgeable class. Now, among the streetwise types, they weren't particularly interested in the knowledgeable part. They were interested in not being anybody's fool. For those who definitely bought into the materialist ideas, the ultimate put-down would be not being able to afford something your friends could have. To have to say, "No, I can't afford it," to have to gulp and say that--that was the bottom of the barrel for some people.

MYRA: The Jews viewed Gentiles as not being as financially responsible and savvy, summed up in the expression *goyische kop,* or "Gentile head"! We once saw a billboard that said, "Jesus Saves," and someone had added "Moses Invests." That was the message of *goyische kop.* The irony, Rog, is that you bought into that. I didn't.

ROGER: Well, I got enough exposure to it at Fairfax High that I kind of understood where it was at. There was that great sea of middle-class *goyim* who lived in tract houses and fought and drank; the idea was not to get trapped in that scene. And the way you got trapped, of course, was you got knocked up! That's the trap! Getting knocked up! If you become a party person you get knocked up, and then you're trapped. *That's* the idea of *goyische kop.*

MYRA: See, I never understood that. I didn't see that.

ROGER: That was the progression: party, knocked up, trapped.

MYRA: I thought, party, fun, cool people, excitement. But guys became cool through their own actions and girls became cool through dating cool guys, through who we went out with.

ROGER: That's right. Guys had a lot more moves than girls did.

MYRA: *We* had a very limited world; it's true. And before you married Mr. Cool, before that, it was being the daughter of thus-and-such family.

ROGER: Yes.

MYRA: You were always a person by association.

ROGER: Women were the ornaments.

MYRA: Although not entirely, even then. While that was enough for some guys, others appreciated a girl who was friendly and intelligent. You liked the fact that you could talk to me, that I was smart.

ROGER: Well, there were a lot of women, a lot of girls, who I had casual affairs with, who were such complete airheads that there wasn't anything to do with them except have sex! And, over time, I got the impression--because it was there in the culture and these were reinforcements of it--that women were simply playthings, that girls were simply for a good time.

MYRA: That they weren't interested in talking.

ROGER: If you wanted intellectual stimulation, you hung out with your friends. But it was reinforced by these *bimbos* that I would go out with, these *airheads*--

MYRA: But we leaned into *acting like* airheads! Some of us. I consciously acted silly. I still enjoy being playful and silly.

ROGER: Myra's right. It was self-reinforcing. The airhead thing, that's what guys expected girls to be.

MYRA: *My algebra teacher wrote that in my yearbook!* She wrote in my ninth grade yearbook, "To a girl who's smart enough not to let the boys know it." She probably saw me as this lucky young thing who had a lot of boyfriends, and that I was smart enough to keep it under my hat that I was smarter than a lot of guys. But there it is in print!
   I was going to say something else about friendships among boys versus those among girls. When we were going out, the first few years, even after we knew we were going to get married, Friday night was like this sacred night that Roger was going to have with the boys. And he never wanted to make any plans to do anything with me. Because he wanted to have that option of spending Friday night with the boys. Whereas, I didn't have any such arrangement that I was going to spend an evening with my girlfriends. I didn't have the commitment to my girlfriends that he had to his boyfriends! And that, I think, is an important point. I very early transferred all my allegiance to the guy that I liked, and my girlfriends could just--well, jump in a lake. That's it, pretty much. It wasn't very nice of me.

ROGER: Well, you know, that's one thing that women's liberation has done. And that's a good thing.

MYRA: Yeah, it was badly needed.

ROGER: It has given women the idea, the legitimacy of having a circle of women friends who are concerned with women's concerns. And, of course, women's concerns are not just getting married and having babies anymore. So the idea of going out with the girls--back in our day, going out with the girls was organized around little standard *shticks*. Among the wealthier girls, there was charity work. Okay? Teas.   And there were various other kinds of "women's activities" that the gals would participate in.   It wasn't the same as going out with the guys!

The guys would call up: "What's happening?" "Ah, I dunno, I'll come by and pick ya up and we'll do something." Okay? And we'd go out cruising, we'd go down Sunset Boulevard, look for girls, see if there was a party anyplace. Sometimes we'd just end up, two of us, Barry and I, or John Farhood and I, or Mel and I, we'd just drive someplace and park. And talk. Till three in the morning. Just talk about any Goddamn thing--sports, girls, cars, philosophy, whatever.

MYRA: I could do that with Sue, but I didn't have a little gang that I'd always check in with to see what was happening.   I really was doing everything, basically, from being involved with *you*. From the time I met you, that was *it*. You know? And I don't know if that was true for every girl, but certainly it was true for a lot of girls. You planned your life around what your boyfriend was doing--when he washed his *car,* or whatever!

I pretty much planned *everything* around what was happening with Roger. And you know the other thing about all this. You want me to say it? That other thing was that women in those days regarded one another, so often, as just competitors, for guys.

7

Sue

Sue, the daughter of a Jewish mother and a Gentile father, found herself forced to choose an identity in order to participate in high school club activities. With her Northern European looks and family ambivalence toward addressing Jewish heritage, Sue became a member of Vogue, the top Gentile girls' club at L.A. High. Yet Sue is remembered by others primarily for her status as an intellectual, a rebel, and a risk-taker, not as a student who embraced "passing."

In the parlance of the day, Sue was also a "fast" girl, whose sharp intelligence and desire to challenge convention made her an influential friend to Myra and Pat. Sue's perspectives on the frustrating high school years address limitations on knowledge and its uses, and her own choice to move beyond Vogue into a broader framework of world politics.

This interview took place in a small restaurant near the West L.A. neighborhood where I was born.

A group of girls called me up in the middle of the night and said, "You have to choose. Are you going to be Christian or Jewish? Because you have to choose in order to rush, and both the Christian and Jewish clubs want you. So what's it going to be?" Ah!

Today is more than forty years later. Perhaps we were clearly products of our families and our environments and what we were exposed to, at that time. Some of us instinctively knew there was more. But I think that would happen anywhere, in any time frame.

We were as unprepared to get married as we were to understand world politics. We lacked information on a grand scale, and we didn't know it. Some of us suspected it.   And those whose parents were doctors and lawyers had a much better grounding and a much better chance. But that's true today; that was true a hundred years ago. So we're talking about class distinctions here. We're talking about growing up in a family that tells you that there is a world and shows it to you.

Perhaps the best illustration is that my parents thought it was a big deal if they took me to Santa Barbara. With my own son, after studying French for a year in high school he went to France! In his lifetime his father took him all over the world, wherever he went to prepare oil leases or to negotiate for governments. He always took him, whether there was school or not. So now my son thinks nothing of traveling anywhere in the world, grabbing a passport, going through customs, speaking languages, communicating in other fields and in other philosophies. It made him become a citizen of the planet.

Now, in our time there were certainly children like that. But we didn't know them. They went to private school. Very few of them passed through the portals of where we were going to high school.

The ones [at L.A. High] who had brains and/or came from fairly affluent families climbed out and became somebody, whether or not they had their parents' blessings. Look at Roger. Roger got up and went and did something wonderful and took Myra with him. And when Myra looked around and said, *"I can too,"* she did. And is. Perhaps the smart ones all did that. But the "smart ones" from that time, we are so disconnected. I mean, we'll never know the end of the story, because we don't see each other, the other gals. And I won't talk about that on the tape recorder because that's a private world.

When you go to college and you join a sorority, those people become the basis of your business and social networking for your lifetime. That's very important. Our parents didn't tell us that. My parents did everything they could to keep me *out* of that. In their ignorance. Which is unfortunate.

I think that's a function of my upbringing. My Jewish mother was so frightened of the fact that I should be polluted by a club or a sorority that she did everything she could to keep me out of it, which was a mistake! But by high school she couldn't do anything about anything I did. She didn't want me to be Jewish. And I joined a Christian club. Only because they were not as restrictive. They didn't *insist* that you only be friends with your own kind. And I had gone on since junior high school upsetting apple carts, befriending people who were not my own kind, and I've continued to do this throughout my life. My very best friend right now is a Japanese lady who lives in Hawaii, and my godson is Japanese. But that friendship, when it began in college, was almost squashed. Both sets of parents said "You cannot be friends with her." Because we were in an environment where there were five races and they were all politely ignoring each other. Our friendship was not acceptable. This, of course, made us friends for life.

I've never been subject to any kind of restrictive rules. But then, I'm a rebel.

So when a group of girls called me up in the middle of the night and said, "You have to decide whether you're going to be Jewish or Christian," I said,

"What are the options?" My reactions, even though I didn't know it, were that of a diplomat. What is to be gained here, for the greater good, by participating in this? At all? And how can we let more light into this closed room? How can I open more windows? To this day I still do walk in and get accepted in places where they think I'm somebody else. And I go open more windows.

They only wanted me because at the beginning of high school I had run for an office, to split an election, because I didn't like who was running and I wanted us to have some unknown human from some other place who was not a snot! Because the leading candidate was very small-minded and a snot, in my opinion. At the time I thought we could benefit by having more windows opened. So I ran, to split this election. But I missed: I got elected! Ha ha! My skills were not polished yet in terms of international diplomacy. That made me class president in the tenth grade, for the girls. I don't know if the boys had a class president; I don't remember. But the person who had that position diplomatically became the person that all the clubs wanted. Because that person was a plum, in terms of student politics. So we were rushed by everybody.

That was why they came and said to me, "You must decide, because all the clubs want you. And whatever side you choose, they will all bid you." Which is when my friends said, "Please choose what *we* want. You don't want to join anything, so what difference does it make to you? We want this desperately and if you go with us we'll get it." So I said, "All right. We'll try it for a year. And if we don't like it--if you like it but I don't like it--I'll blow it up."

The club was named Vogue. And I couldn't have told you that a year ago, until your mother came back and started talking about these people. And when she first started talking, the girls were words: the names were Vogue names that I'd heard, but I couldn't put faces to them. Because it was so far back in the cotton wool of my mind.

The reasons [for receiving a bid to Vogue, the top Christian girls' club] were all very shallow reasons; they were the product of a lack of knowledge. Lack of understanding. Lack of communication! That was the problem. And I *fought* to go to L.A. High School because my mother taught at Hollywood High School, and the other two high schools, Hamilton and Fairfax, were all one denomination. They were 99 percent Jewish. I wanted to go someplace where there was a little bit of everybody. And I had to take three buses every morning to do that.

But look, if you will, at the history of civilizations. Yugoslavia is now demonstrating exactly the same thing, they are doing exactly the same thing on a world scale: everyone saying, "We want to be with *our own kind.* " This is inherent in people. People in their ignorance want to be with what they're familiar with. They want to go back and return to what they know, what they grew up with, what they were taught, what they learned their first survival skills in. Unless, of course, you educate them. Which is why we all give our dollars to UCLA for scholarships so they can educate more kids.

What was Vogue like? There was rushing. The girls that were the seniors at that time were the last group of civilized, educated girls from good families that I remember, who went to college. The girl that was my big sister went to Stanford, which made sense to me because my family went to Stanford. So I was just barely oriented. That girl was not prejudiced, she was a normal person. Mostly, after that, there were only *two* of us in the entire club that kept up our grade-point average, for the club, because that was not impressive. It was important to be blond and blue-eyed and good-looking; *that's* what they valued. It's why I remember so little. I was dating a midshipman who went to Annapolis. My priorities were different than theirs. The other fellow I was dating went to Stanford. They [the Vogues] seemed silly; I didn't pay a lot of attention.

There were functions like teas that were a part of rushing. If those functions could have been construed positively they would have prepared you for college rushing, which was far more intense and far more prejudicial; far more deadly. But useful. Had we had any knowledge, had we had any direction--had *I* had any direction either in school or at home, I would have accomplished much more. To go through all of this and then grow up to be a discussion leader for the League of Women Voters is truly laughable. To look back and see how provincial we were: our enormous lack of information, which was overwhelming! But I think that's a function of my family. I really do. And the men, too, were the products of their families. But the brighter they were, the more they would *seek* knowledge. If you're bright and you're active, you go out and fall over things and become involved. And that takes you farther and farther away from this little tiny experience.

I mean, the whole experience of Vogue was so *trivial!* Who could have been scared of those people? Who could have been in any way *hindered* by those women? Children! They weren't women; they were kids.

It meant something to them, that good grooming. What I don't remember is that information being used positively, as in how to prepare for social situations in the world. Think if we had been able to capture, and harness, the positive aspects of all that debutante business. If we had had some kind of decent parenting and knowledgeable people! I think there were many opportunities that we were not aware of, and we could have learned a *lot* more, earlier, if we had had a little help. And I can only compare it to raising my son and watching him and his contemporaries achieve many, many things. And I'm sure Myra and I and the others are now very, very aware that we make our life; we make our destinies. I don't think we knew it then. We're all independent now, none of us works from nine to five for anybody. If the town burned down tomorrow I could pick up my gym bag and walk out of here and make a life somewhere else. And survive and make money on my own, with my wits. And I think Myra and Roger could too.

While I was in Vogue I expressed my opinions; yes, I did, to their great disgust. As in any organization, you can't make any changes until you have leverage. You have to have been there long enough; you have to have enough seniority. So you have to bide your time and then, when you *have* some leverage, you can gently move things around and change the dominoes on the board. That's what I did. It didn't make a lot of difference because some of them were just lumps of clay! They were not interested in *anything* besides looking good. I'm sure they all grew up to be great wives, and were married five years and had 2.3 kids and got a divorce. That 0.3 kid is always the interesting one.

The Vogue rush system, as with systems in the Jewish sororities, excluded probably 75 per cent of the young ladies in school. I can't remember--maybe Helen or Myra could tell you what percentage of girls got involved in clubs. But the point is that the percentage of girls that did *not* get involved in this and *knew* about it were *hurt* by it, because they weren't included. And you're talking children here; they wanted to belong. They went on into college, a lot of them, wanting to belong. And went through the same thing all over again! Because no matter who you thought you were, or how good your self-image was, to be rejected by these kids who supposedly had some kind of power or claim was very painful. And I kind of thought that was *unnecessary.* I didn't think much of that, *at all.*

At that time nonwhite students didn't want to be members of the white clubs. They had their own little cliques. But were there clubs for Asian or black students? No one ever asked. Because *nobody knew them.* By then we had been weaned. We were weaned, early, by our parents; at least, I was. I remember the first black kid I tried to bring home from Scout camp, to play. I had it all set up--until my mother found out she was black. And said, "I am sorry, you will have to cancel this engagement." "Why?" I asked. "Well, because we don't mix." My mother lost a lot of points that day. But I must have been in grammar school then. So by the time I was in high school I knew that was a battle I couldn't win yet. You need more leverage, for that one. Ultimately, I've had my leverage. I've raised a child who writes for television and changes the minds of many people, and knows and cares about whether what he writes changes people.

But you must look at history. At that time, in the Ivy League school system, the same thing was going on times ten, in a logarithmic progression, much more intense. I mean, the California schools were *laid back* compared to what went on back east in terms of clubs and schools and the power that is still going on.

A lot of them [in Vogue] liked what they had. They wouldn't have changed it because they couldn't imagine what else they could have. In order to give up what you think you have at the top of the heap, you have to be able to imagine something better; there has to be something out there that's a brighter star. Maybe you have to be born knowing that you're a citizen of the world. That's something I've know since I was very small, first or second grade. I remember knowing at a very early age that my mother was showing me how *not* to do things. And that that was all she knew. She showed me how *not* to do it. Because she didn't know *how* to do it. She would do something, or make a decision, that was wrong, and I would see that it was wrong. But I didn't have any leverage. So I'd mark it. I'd mark teachers in school who would do the same thing. I'd say, No, this isn't the right answer. The fact that I could hear their thoughts, or know what they were going to do, gave me an advantage that most people didn't have. But because of it I knew there was more. I knew somehow, somewhere, there was more! I always knew that!

My mother, in her desire to protect me, probably in her desire to keep me from being hurt, tried to keep me in a closed, provincial world, probably as a result of the world *she* grew up in. When she grew up, girls were not supposed to go to college. But she did. She went and got a master's degree in math. Her sister went and got a doctorate in psychology. My mother taught school all her life and her sister became a guidance counselor after teaching at the University of Hawaii. Both of them went to college in the Depression, during a time when their father, without telling anybody, lost his business and lost his house! The first thing they knew about it was when somebody knocked on the door and told them to move out! They took their mother and they moved out of the house. They left their father standing there--only because they were so annoyed that he hadn't bothered to warn them this was coming.

She was scared. My mother ran on fear. Fear of everything. She had a self-image of minus seven; thought she was as homely as a mud fence. And she ran on fear. By the time I joined a non-Jewish club my mother and I didn't talk. We lived in an armed camp. We inhabited the same house, but there was no communication in it; none at all. Nor was there any guidance--or any warmth. That's probably why I needed all those boyfriends.

All my life I've never known what anybody else thought of me. That's a blind spot. I know what *Myra* thought. But I loved her. I know what my friend Lynn thought, too, but I loved her: her mother brought me up. Lynn had a mother like Auntie Mame. She was a designer for California Jewelsmiths in Beverly Hills. She looked beautiful, stopping-a-train-magnificent. Not beautiful features, but she knew what to do with what she had; she dressed beautifully. It's hard to judge Mother; if she walked into a room she would have been judged the most striking woman in the room, instantly. Everyone would have deferred to her because of the way she was: her presence. That woman taught me to dress!

When I came back from grad school, my husband joined a Beverly Hills firm. It wasn't what we had planned to happen, but we had to eat. He was still studying for the California bar; he was a member of the bar in Texas and a couple of other places but not here. So here we were. The firm wanted him because he was an oil and gas lawyer: they didn't have that, and besides he was international and they didn't have that. But they had their foot on his neck because he had to pass the bar and we were babies. So our first major hurdle was the Jefferson Jackson Day Dinner for President Johnson. Right after Kennedy was assassinated, there was this huge hundred dollars a plate dinner for Johnson, to raise money so he could get the world together. And of course the firm had some tables at this. Well, to go to this! I mean this was *black tie,* thank you very much, with jewels and clothes and oh-my-God. A man doesn't have a problem because he can rent a tux and he's immediately all right. But with a woman: I mean it isn't a matter of knowing *what* to do; it's a matter of coming up with the money to do it. At that time in life I did not have any idea that I was an artist. I had had that beaten out of me when I was very small. But I basically got in there and made a dress. And a coat, a floor-length coat. And I went over to Lynn's mom and said, Help. Shoes, jewels, diamonds, purses, all the accessories, and I went to the dinner. I didn't say a word; I didn't know enough about international world politics at that point. I had gotten as far as grad school and international commerce by then, so I knew a little bit. But I knew enough to know that I didn't know enough; I knew enough to know that I was dumb. But because I kept still, *they* didn't know I didn't know. Which has always been my ace. And I knew *that* before I got to Vogue.

The art of conversation I learned in grad school, from Europeans, who thought Americans were terminally tedious. These same guys were my volleyball partners and we played two-man killer volleyball; I was the only woman in the school that played. We talked. We talked about everything in the world. They were an education, those men. We were still kids, but we weren't kids; we were twenty-two.

I wish I could say I had good teachers at L.A. High. There was one human. He was head of the Math Department. He understood that if somebody didn't protect me and help me I would probably blow up the school. That man--maybe he did know my mother and maybe that's why he did it. I was a math major, daughter of a math major, see? I got straight A's and didn't take anything else because why bother. I didn't know I was an artist. That guy let me correct papers and work in his office one period a day. Except I was never there. I was at UCLA in the library; I was at the beach; I was anywhere but in that school. And that man covered my fanny. That man and your mother's access to every piece of paper in the school.

Myra was head of the girls' Senior Board, or whatever, and that allowed her to walk in and out of every principal's office and the attendance office. And it allowed her to send her minions to those places. She never knew. She had no idea that I had a form file, and everytime somebody fucked up and left campus and couldn't get back into school I wrote them a note and got them back, including me. You just needed little pieces of paper about that big. I've told Myra about that. It wasn't women rebelling; it was brains rebelling. The gender didn't matter.

There aren't very many people in every class who are very bright and who are diplomats. There aren't a lot of diplomats in the world; if there were, the world would work better. Most of the diplomats get sucked, early, into the intelligence services. And if we had been boys, we would be there too. Earlier. And they run the world from behind the scenes because most people are not quick enough to understand the implications of what goes on globally. High school was like that for me;   I understood so much more than I could *do*. To understand the restrictions put on people was to allow them to overcome those restrictions; in other words, the people who tried to break out for the most part were bright. And mishandled. Kids who weren't bad; they were bored. They were "taught." If our high school had not run at the rate of the average I wouldn't have cut school. I would have done something. And I was surrounded by people like that.

I didn't have any idea that I was a forger, because I didn't know that I was an artist. But I could look at a signature once and copy it because I'm a calligrapher! And I'm good at it! But I didn't know it then; I didn't have a clue. So all I did was run interference, for me or for anybody else who was bored to the teeth. I mean these weren't kids who were out selling drugs. These weren't kids who were out robbing houses. These were kids who wanted to go to a library at some other college to find out something, or who wanted to get out because they were so bored they didn't know what to do. Mostly I wasn't connected to the people there; my connections were outside the school.

Myra thought she was helping. She sure didn't do student government for glory or because she thought she was better than anyone. She did it because she thought, somehow, she could make a contribution. She had the world's best intentions. If she had understood why I was doing what I was doing, she would have probably cheered, instead of being horrified. She never found out about it because she *would* have been horrified. It would have blown her out of the saddle. I got away with a lot, a very great deal. Because I would always put on my pith helmet and wander into somebody else's culture and sit down and have coffee with them. Find out what they did; what they were about. But we were not encouraged to go into the black culture, into the Spanish culture, and they wouldn't come near us. At my high school there was no social concept of that. We were so conditioned by then.

I wish I could tell you more about what they did in Vogue, and what went on with them, but most of them were asleep. I mean, the sad fact is that much of the world is the Roman mob.

I didn't quit because I could do more by staying, by being in there. I could counter more stuff by staying. And in order to function in that school, I had to have a boyfriend in that school for cover. I led a multifaceted life, designed to survive and keep the peace in that school. Because I knew that that school would come to an end, and I would go on into the future and never see these people again. Somehow, I would go beyond the rainbow. Have you ever felt that way, in school? Did you feel that, too?

Afterword

Just remember, we're all in this alone.

--Lily Tomlin

For the title of his 1976 book, writer Ralph Keyes asked the question "Is there life after high school?" His suggestion that we youth-oriented Americans retain, throughout adult life, the reputations and status we carve for ourselves in adolescence is surely terrifying to some, flattering to others. What is remarkable is the mood of *anxiety*--and its evil twin, embarassment--created by the journey back into high school nostalgia.

How did the participants in this oral history project, all but two of whom have known me since my infancy, respond to seeing their memories writ large? My mother, Myra, remarked that in these interviews she and her friends all reverted to their high school way of speaking. After reading her own sections of the manuscript, she wrote to me:

I thought again about the plight of all immigrants and their dilemma with their kids: wanting to assimilate and yet knowing this means a certain loss of cultural identity. This was so familiar and clear to me when I read Amy Tan's books, and again when I thought about the probable differences in Jewish kids going to Fairfax versus L.A. High. I don't think we had any of these identity crises in junior high, where we were *not* a minority; but now we are still dealing with the identity issue in our lives.

Several of the participants were sufficiently aghast, after proofreading their own recollections, to ask that I change their names and certain other identifying characteristics, citing concerns for their current professional stature.   Others negotiated not only with me but with family members before agreeing to publication. My parents consulted with one another, and, by telephone, with all of the other participants to determine which casual comments from the original interviews might be hurtful in print. As a result of these editorial concerns, even more perspectives on the 1950s were forthcoming, old friendships kindled anew, and my ancient role as "Myra and Roger's little girl" vanished forevermore into my new persona as the historical dominatrix in need of signed release forms.

In response to Keyes's question, yes, there is indeed life after high school. Without shattering too many privacies, I can avow that all of the participants grew up to be successful in their chosen work. Myra is a popular children's dance teacher. Roger recently retired after more than twenty years as an air quality policy analyst for the Department of Energy. Pat is a private therapist. Sue is an artist working with the California Renaissance Fair. Bob, Helen, and Jennifer are hard-working and creative professionals still living in Southern California.

Altogether, the participants speaking herein have raised twelve children.

This child, in particular, is grateful for the opportunity to preserve a time gone by. We might all strive to serve as our own biographers, for there is no greater joy than a group of friends challenging and corroborating their shared, authentic American past, whatever the subcultural text might be.   And there was, in this work, a personal pleasure for me, in acting on the ancient obligation of kibud av, "Honor thy mother and father."

                                                    Bonnie J. Morris
                                                    1996/5757

Recommended Readings

Armor, John, and Peter Wright. *Manzanar.* Times Books, 1988.

Bailey, Beth. *From Front Porch to Back Seat: Courtship Rituals in Twentieth Century America.* John Hopkins University Press, 1988.

Baum, Charlotte, Paula Hyman and Sonya Michel. *The Jewish Woman in America.* New American Library, 1975.

Breines, Winifred. *Young, White, and Miserable: Growing Up Female in the Fifties.* Beacon, 1992.

Cassady, Carolyn. *Off the Road: My Life with Jack Kerouac.* William Morrow, 1990.

Doherty, Thomas. *Teenagers and Teenpics: The Juvenilization of American Movies in the 1950s.* Unwin Hyman, 1988.

Douglas, Susan. *Where the Girls Are: Growing Up Female with the Mass Media.* Times Books, 1994.

Ehrenreich, Barbara. *The Hearts of Men.* Anchor, 1983.

Farina, Richard. *Been Down So Long It Looks Like Up to Me.* Random House, 1966.

Farnham, Marynia, and Ferdinand Lundberg. *Modern Woman: The Lost Sex.* Grosset and Dunlap, 1947.

Gaar, Gillian. *She's a Rebel: The History of Women in Rock and Roll.* Seal Press, 1992.

Gluck, Sherna Berger. *Rosie the Riveter Revisited: Women, the War, and Social Change.* New American Library, 1987.

Head, Gay. *Hi There, High School!* Scholastic Books, 1953.

Kerouac, Jack. *The Dharma Bums.* c.1958. Penguin, 1976.

Keyes, Ralph. *Is There Life After High School?* Little, Brown, 1976.

Lord, M.C. *Forever Barbie.* William Morrow, 1994.

Mauldin, Bill. *Back Home.* W. Sloan Associates, 1947.

May, Elaine Tyler. *Homeward Bound: American Families in the Cold War Era.* Basic Books, 1988.

McKown, Harry. *School Clubs: Their Organization, Administration, Supervision and Activities.* Macmillan, 1929.

Meyerowitz, Joanne, ed. *Not June Cleaver.* Temple University Press, 1994.

Namias, June. *First Generation.* Beacon, 1978.

Palladino, Grace. *Teenagers: An American History.* HarperCollins, 1996.

Rippey, Stewart George. *The Year of the Oath: The Fight for Academic Freedom at the University of Southern California.* Doubleday, 1950.

Rogin, Michael. *Blackface, White Noise: Jewish Immigrants in the Hollywood Melting Pot.* University of California Press, 1996.

Roiphe, Anne. *Generation Without Memory. Beacon,* 1982.

Shulman, Alix Kates. *Memoirs of an Ex-Prom Queen.* Knopf, 1972.

Smith, Lillian. *Killers of the Dream.* W.W. Norton, 1949.

Solinger, Rickie. *Wake Up Little Susie: Single Pregnancy and Race Before Roe v. Wade.* Routledge, 1992.

Steiner, Dale. *Of Thee We Sing: Immigrants and American History.* Harcourt Brace Jovanovich, 1987.

Takei, George. *To the Stars.* Pocket Books, 1994.

Timmons, Stuart. *The Trouble with Harry Hay.* Alyson, 1990.

Wilentz, Elias, ed. *The Beat Scene.* Corinth, 1960.

Wylie, Philip. *Generation of Vipers.* Farrar and Rinehart, 1942.

Yezierska, Anzia. *The Bread Givers.* Persea Books, 1975.

Index

About the Author

BONNIE J. MORRIS is a Visiting Assistant Professor of Women's Studies at George Washington University.

ISBN 0-89789-494-4

HARDCOVER BAR CODE